A WORLD TO GAIN

A WORLD TO GAIN

Incarnation and the Hope of Renewal

Brian Horne

Darton, Longman and Todd
London

First published in 1983
Darton, Longman and Todd Ltd
89 Lillie Road
London SW6 1UD

© Brian Horne 1983

ISBN 0 232 51543 3

British Library Cataloguing in Publication Data

Horne, Brian
  A world to gain.
  1. Christian life
  I. Title
  248.4   BV4501.2

  ISBN 0–232–51543–3

Phototypeset by Input Typesetting Ltd,
London SW19 8DR
Printed in Great Britain by
Richard Clay (The Chaucer Press) Ltd
Bungay, Suffolk

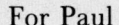
For Paul

CHRIST IS OUR PEACE

This book is the third in a series of three focusing on Catholic Renewal in the Church of England using the central theme 'Christ is Our Peace'. The first volume by Michael Hollings is entitled *Hearts Not Garments* (DLT 1982) and deals with renewal of the Christian. The second volume by Richard Holloway is entitled *Signs of Glory* (DLT 1982) and deals with renewal and the faith of the Church. This volume by Brian Horne deals with the renewal of the world. It is hoped that the books will be read by all Christians interested in renewal, regardless of denomination.

CONTENTS

ACKNOWLEDGEMENT

The Scripture quotations in this publication are from the Revised Standard Version of the Bible, copyrighted 1971 and 1952 by the Division of Christian Education of the National Council of the Churches of Christ in the U.S.A.

PROLOGUE

Only the Hebrew-Christian tradition could have produced the Communist Manifesto; Karl Marx's revolutionary call to arms is accompanied by a resoundingly confident promise about the future: 'Let the governing classes tremble before the communist revolution. The proletarians have nothing to lose but their chains. They have the whole world to gain.' The belief that history is not a meaningless succession of events, 'a tale/Told by an idiot, full of sound and fury,/Signifying nothing', but something which moves purposefully forward to a future which holds the promise of a better life is a belief that Karl Marx derived from the religions that had shaped Western civilization. The characteristic stance of Jews and Christians alike is one of expectancy: hope for the future in a new world. Nor does the similarity between Judaism, Christianity and Marxism end there despite the fact that the kind of world that is hoped for, and the means by which it will be attained, diverge substantially. The many and various messianic expectations of Judaism have always, in some way or other (some mystical, some practical), revolved around the city of Jerusalem and the vindication of God's chosen people. The Marxist hope has been strictly secular: the eradication of injustice, the freeing of the enslaved, the establishment of the classless society; in short the realization, in history, of a utopian dream. It is easy to see where the Christian hope for the future runs parallel to, and overlaps with, these expectations. It shares with Judaism the symbol of Jerusalem, this image of the 'city': a perfect association of man with man living under the power of God inspires and troubles the

1

Christian imagination. It shares with Marxism, despite its many failures in practice, the determination to establish freedom and justice. But the Christian hope for the new world is both simpler and more complicated. It is more complicated because it is not merely utopian but also supernatural, and the interlocking of the two spheres is not easily discernible. It is simpler because it perceives that there is but one means by which the new world is to be gained: the power of God in Jesus Christ. Any book, therefore, about the renewal of the world will have the figure of Christ at its centre, for if we do not know him we cannot know what to expect.

However, I do not want to turn this into an exercise in Christology; it is meant, after all, to be a book about the world. I am simply warning in advance that a book which dares to approach the subject will also have to be a book about God. His action of creation and redemption has made the world part of his own story. The destiny of mankind, and indeed of the whole material universe, is, as I hope I shall show, only to be found within the life of God himself. The world which will be gained is a world which will be seen to be divine. Caught between memory and expectation, the now and the not-yet, the Christian tries to build the 'just city' of the now while seeking the heavenly Jerusalem of the not-yet; but he can do the former only because of his search for the latter.

Chapter 1

THE WORLD OF THE INDIVIDUAL

The human condition

The life of modern man is dominated by a paradox. On the one hand he is conscious, as never before, of his power. The scientific and technological achievements of the last two centuries have given him an awareness of control over the material universe that has made him see both himself and that universe in a new perspective. A new relationship now exists between man and the world he inhabits. The conception of earlier ages of a cosmos in which each particle of animate and inanimate matter occupied a preordained place in a vast and intricate but discernible pattern—and remained occupying its proper place until the dissolution of the universe and the restoration of all things at the Second Coming—was destroyed long before our present century, though the implications of the destruction of that notion have, perhaps, filtered down to all levels of society only in the present century. The pattern began to disintegrate as early as the seventeenth century, when scientific discoveries suggested new patterns, or no pattern at all.

The collapse of the notion of the fixed order of the cosmos called into question the notion of God as creator and deeply affected the way man thought about himself. It is hardly surprising that the remarkable achievements of scientists and engineers in the nineteenth century should greatly increase man's sense of his own importance and implant an optimism in his heart with the promise of a better future which was waiting to be born when, scientifically, the time was right. 'That future, in view of man's achievements during the period of his known history, was conceived of as full of unlimited possibilities for further advance' (E. L. Elliott-Binns, p. 28). Despite the fact that many scientists in the nineteenth century remained Christians, science could be seen to be parting company with religion. Traditional Christian hopes for the future were

> repudiated by the ardent minds of the new scientific era. The golden age which they foresaw was to be realised here on earth and it would owe nothing to any supernatural guidance or help; man's own efforts, wisely directed by reason and informed by the new knowledge, would suffice and bring it into being (ibid).

The scientific and technological advances have continued in the twentieth century into areas and in ways which seem almost miraculous to ordinary men and women who wake each day to the news of some further probe into space or another organ transplant. Man's ability to explore the hitherto mysterious universe which surrounds his planet has been paralleled by his capacity to investigate and reorganize the physical and chemical constitutents of that same planet. He can alter the shape and development of his environment and even his own species at will. The potentialities of life and the possibilities of what could be achieved seem to stretch before him excitingly and endlessly.

That is only half of the picture. When the coin of contemporary life is turned to its reverse side a contradictory scene is shown and the weight of the paradox is felt. In spite of all that has been accomplished and all that can be prognosticated, the human race lives under a cloud of intense anxiety; the darkest mood, often encountered, is one of total despair. The great achievements of science and technology which seem to hold out the promise of an enhanced quality of life at the same time threaten that life with hideous destruction and impose moral burdens that weigh down the spirit. The very power that now lies within human grasp seems only to emphasize human frailty and weakness. The inability to resolve the moral dilemmas of his existence drives into man's heart

4

the apparent meaninglessness of that existence. He is constantly confronted by the seeming impossibility of preventing the destructive potentialities from becoming actualities in the violence and fear which characterize the contemporary world.

Of course, man's desolate cry about his own frailty and the futility of existence is no new thing: the history of Western literature has many examples of nihilistic protest, but never before has the expression of hopelessness and fearful bewilderment been so universal; and when twentieth-century man has turned to art for inspiration and consolation he has been given, by the greatest of the artists, images of chaos and destruction, portrayals of the dissolution of all that has been secure and stable. It is often said that the folly and destruction of the First World War caused the shadow of despair and loss to fall across European civilization, but the finest imaginations had already sensed the anxiety creeping coldly into the marrow of the bones of human life. Before the horrors of that war were known T. S. Eliot had written,

> Wipe your hand across your mouth, and laugh;
> The worlds revolve like ancient women
> Gathering fuel in vacant lots.

(Preludes, IV)

This image of futility presaged the literature of despair, sometimes cynical, sometimes angry, which grew in the years following 1918. If the Christian is to answer the despair of the world and speak about its renewal without being dismissed as trivial, he is obliged to face the question it poses about meaning in its most serious and challenging form.

Such a serious challenge came in the writings of Albert Camus. The paradox I have been speaking about was described precisely by Camus when he referred to 'our miserable and magnificent existence'. He managed to voice the sense of the alienation and isolation of the individual as almost no one else did; the meaninglessness of existence in a world in which one could find neither religious nor political commitment. He saw that these two forms of idealism could, if anything could, provide a purpose for the individual, and he pondered on the religious question constantly. But what if, as appeared to be the case with most people, religious and political commitment eluded one? He posed the questions with such vividness and accuracy that he seemed to be speaking to everyone in their darker moments when he wrote in 1938: 'There is but one truly serious philosophical problem and that is suicide. Judging whether life is or is not worth living amounts to answering the fundamental questions of philosophy' (*The Myth of Sisyphus*, p. 7). Contemplating this question he evolved, as many others were doing and have been doing since, a 'philosophy' of the 'absurd'. This way of thinking pierces the armour of Christian defences and forces the Christian to ask again what kind of creature man is and what kind of God it is in whom he professes belief.

For Christianity to remain true to its eschatological character and, at the same time, to speak to this age offering individuals a world in which they might find meaning, it must take into account this prevailing paradox. It must indicate ways in which the Christian understanding of God and man offers a possible reconciliation of man's confidence in himself and his appalling anxiety. Just as the programmes offered by Liberal Protestantism in nineteenth-century Europe were shattered by the violence of twentieth-century warfare, so the numerous reductionist attempts at 'humanizing' God and eliminating the transcendental element in Christian faith seem inadequate in the present situation. This attempted demystification of religion has been working with only one half of a true concept of man and has missed the point of Camus's powerful complaint against life: the impenetrability of its mystery. The attempt to answer Camus's question about suicide, then, cannot be based upon the kind of 'religionless Christianity' which is centred upon admiration for and imitation of the life of Jesus of Nazareth. Turning faith into morals is not going to come to grips with the fact of the mystery.

The first stage in this process, and the first step in Christian maturity, is the recognition that the mystery is supernatural and that the destiny of man is a supernatural destiny. In

6

making this statement I am aware of the immediate danger of being misunderstood. I do not mean to imply that the Christian's understanding of life is irrational or that the world he inhabits is under the control of forces from 'outside' which can only be invoked and manipulated by magical means. Still less am I suggesting that the answers to the questions man asks about himself can only be given after death in 'heaven': a realm of the supernatural that is totally other than the one in which he now lives and tries to find meaning. Such a view of the radical separation of natural and supernatural, though frequently presented to gullible minds as the truth by both Quietist and Apocalypticist preachers, is a perversion of the Christian gospel. This can hardly be emphasized too strongly, for the last two decades have seen a disturbing growth of religious sects which have taken as a basic assumption a radical discontinuity between nature and supernature. The appalling community set up by Jim Jones in 'Jonestown', Guyana, in the late 1970s is only one, though admittedly an extreme, example of this. The massacre of hundreds of people which ended the 'experiment' (there is evidence that Jones had warned the world that this event was imminent) can be read as a monstrous acting-out, on the scale of a whole community, of a possible answer to Camus's question about suicide. Life having become intolerable at the natural level in its sheer absurdity, the only solution was a ritual act of self-immolation in the hope that a supernatural existence (for that was what Messiah Jones promised his followers) would give meaning and happiness where a natural existence had failed.

When Charles Williams wrote, 'our common day should relate itself to extraordinary subjects and ends; to glory, to joy, to purity and power', he was putting into plain words the apprehension of the interpenetration of natural and supernatural which is the essence of the Christian doctrine of man. 'So God created man in his own image, in the image of God he created him' (Gen. 1:27). To be made in the image of God is to be made, among other things, for a supernatural purpose and ultimately a supernatural destiny. He is intended to be

7

the inhabitant of a supernatural world which has its beginnings here in the natural world.

In the first volume of his *Theological Investigations* Karl Rahner draws out some of the implications of this doctrine. 'If God gives creation and man above all a supernatural end and this end is first "in intentione", then man (and the world) *is* by that very fact always and everywhere inwardly other in structure than he would be if he did not have this end' (p. 302–3). 'Other in structure.' This is the heart of the matter: man's structure and his destiny are mutually dependent and explain each other. Without the recognition of the destiny that awaits man his structure becomes meaningless. 'In a world without God life becomes absurd; death makes the point' (André Malraux). And without a true apprehension of the structure, the destiny will be misconceived, giving at best only the illusion of hope. 'Hope will be hope for the wrong thing' (T. S. Eliot).

Because man is made in the image of God a fundamental experience is the experience of freedom and the possibility of self-fulfilment; but when the movement forward of man's life is pursued solely at the level of the scientific or the political or the social or the personal, the apparently graspable future turns out to be a void in which the only sound that can be heard is the cry of despair. It is at this moment that man discovers that he cannot be his own absolute future. Nothing satisfies him at the deepest level of personal experience, his world is tragically incomplete and he must be constantly reaching out beyond himself if he is to fulfil his destiny. That destiny is supernatural; it is nothing other than that which has been given by grace already: God.

This is not a discovery of the twentieth century, though our experience of the paradox of the human condition may be more keenly felt. But the essence is there in the *Summa Theologica* when Thomas Aquinas examines the purpose for which man was created and the happiness which is his last end. It is there when he writes that only the sight of God can satisfy the longing gaze of man ('Treatise on the Last End' *S.T.* Pt. ii, qq. i–v). Eight centuries earlier Augustine's famous words from his *Confessions* express the experience with greater emotional intensity: 'Thou God hast made me for Thyself, and my heart is restless until it finds its rest in Thee.' Fifteen hundred years have not robbed the cry of its power. The yearning which is in the heart of man, and which forms the rock out of which all paradise myths have been quarried, has remained stubbornly unchanged despite the acquisition of scientific knowledge and advanced technology. In fact, the centuries of progress have made the living of a human life more problematic and painful because the new knowledge, at first so exciting and full of promise, drives the paradox home more cruelly. There is no middle path of secular optimism between the 'despair' of Camus and the 'hope' of the Christian vision of the world that is to be gained.

That world is to be envisaged neither in terms of the paradise myth, although there has appeared from time to time in Christian literature versions of the myth of innocence restored, nor in terms of apocalyptic foreboding, however often preachers introduce into sermons strains of lurid prophesying about the sudden and violent end of all things. For the most part, Christian eschatology has held fast to the kind of thinking that is expressed, for instance, by St Paul when he writes on these matters to the Christian community in Rome. In the eighth chapter of that epistle he speaks in visionary language about the Christian hope of the world to come.

We know that the whole creation has been groaning in travail together until now; and not only the creation, but we ourselves, who have the first fruits of the Spirit, groan inwardly as we await for adoption as sons, the redemption of our bodies. For in this hope we were saved.

He is agnostic about the details but confident about the substance of this hope. The whole material universe is, furthermore (and this cannot be stressed too strongly), caught up in this process. There are no apocalyptic images to frighten human beings into the hands of God, nor any seductive pictures of Eden to entice them back into a belief in 'dreaming innocence'. An other-worldly existence utterly unlike anything we now know, and a return to a golden age, are both excluded. Admittedly, St Paul's words are enigmatic, but whatever the exact interpretation may be, we can say that what is expected, and expected with serene conviction, is a life in the future which is not radically discontinuous with a life that is lived in the present. However much the present world may be fraught with pain and frustration, the world to come is a transfiguration of what has already begun in man's natural experience. In his natural life his supernatural destiny is already apprehended, not as a kind of compensation for being subject to 'futility', but as a condition of his creation. So his desire for self-transcendence and this reaching out towards it is something done not merely to escape what is also part of his present experience—the pain and limitation of material, earthly existence—but the supernatural spiritual drive of man seeking fulfilment. The reaching out is a reaching forward into the life of God himself.

Are we then to become divine? Is this the end for which man was created, the 'world' he has to gain? In answering Yes to these questions I am immediately conscious of the many and great dangers that lie in my path. There are not many in Western Christianity who have interpreted man's nature and destiny in quite these terms.

First there will be raised the objection that in the account of the Fall in Genesis, sin is described precisely as the attempt by the human race to reach beyond itself, to snatch at and possess that which it did not have, namely, divinity. 'But the serpent said to the woman . . . God knows when you eat of it your eyes will be opened and you will be like God, knowing good and evil.' The ungovernable desire of man to over-reach himself, to be 'as God', refusing his creaturely status, has always been regarded as the 'original' sin, that is the seed from which all evils grow. And it is visited with terrible retribution. Perhaps the most potent of all legends is the Promethean/Faustian legend, and it is based upon the restless dissatisfaction of man with his 'lot' and his desire to be God.

No one understood this better than Martin Luther. When he attempted the purification of Christianity in the sixteenth century he attacked what he regarded as the blasphemous element of hubris in the medieval conception of man's nature and destiny, and set up the antinomy of *Theologia Crucis* and *Theologia Gloriae*. This antinomy is not only central to Luther's thought, it became central to the whole of Protestantism, and we cannot simply set it aside as being of little importance. Even when one has taken into account the context of Luther's thinking and the immediate pressures he was under to formulate such a teaching, it remains one of the most significant insights of Reformation theology. Though I am proposing a *theologia gloriae*—for I can find no other term to describe the process of 'divinization'—it is different from that to which Luther was opposed. There is no element of hubris here, and it is not incompatible with a *theologia crucis*.

I am proposing a theory which sees the process of divinization not as a kind of inevitable evolution in man's history, still less as something which can be achieved by the industrious efforts of man himself. The painful paradox of our condition makes this impossibility plain.

> Between the idea
> And the reality
> Between the motion
> And the act
> Falls the Shadow
> > (T. S. Eliot, *The Hollow Men*).

Between our desires and their fulfilment falls the shadow. It has always been so. The myth of the Fall, as Charles Williams remarked, is less a tale of pride and disobedience than a tale of impossibility. It is impossible for man to turn himself into what he is not. The divinity which is the fulfilment of his nature is not something that can be seized or stolen, as in the legend of Prometheus, nor something which can be bought, as in the legend of Faust. It is a gift of grace: the grace that is conveyed in his being made in the image of his creator. So we begin to see that man's capacity and will to transcend himself (what Karl Rahner calls in a useful shorthand phrase his 'supernatural existential') would remain moribund and

11

ultimately meaningless if the mystery which is God did not communicate itself to that which has it as its destiny. It is therefore in that action of God which is given the name of incarnation and, further, in that particular figure of Jesus Christ that man begins to discover the shape of the world he has to gain. Upon this event the Christian hope for the renewal of the world is founded.

The incarnation as the foundation of renewal

The publication of a collection of essays entitled *The Myth of God Incarnate* was the cause of a furious controversy. It was answered by another collection of essays ineptly called *The Truth of God Incarnate*, as though myth and truth were necessarily mutually exclusive, and a series of publications which charted the course of the debate. Many of the attacks upon the book were ill-conceived, often arising out of wilful misunderstanding or unthinking prejudice, and it is not my intention to examine either the contents of the book or the way in which the ensuing controversy was conducted. The original collection was, in any case, only the most recent attempt of many in the history of the Church to question the historical and philosophical foundations upon which the doctrine of the incarnation has been constructed, and to escape, if possible, from the definitions of the earliest ecumenical councils in which the doctrine had been expressed.

Some of the authors of *The Myth of God Incarnate* seem to have been surprised at the amount of hostility their book aroused. They should not have been; it was, after all, a serious attempt to take a fresh look at the most serious of all Christian assertions: that in the person of Jesus of Nazareth, God became man. Viewed from the stance of a non-Christian this assertion is the most absurd of all dogmas, and it is the dogma in which the scandalous uniqueness of Christianity is most outrageously expressed.

Much of the work of demythologizing theologians is devoted to the examination of the 'records' of the Christian religion, trying to discover whether the original documents and traditions of the Church really do yield up statements like those incarnational formulations of the Nicene creed or the Chalcedonian definition. But behind all the attempts to demythologize the doctrine of the incarnation lie two principles: first, the assumption that the gulf between the twentieth century and earlier ages is so great that the words and images of our ancestors have become opaque and, second, the desire to make the Christian 'reading' of human existence less obscure and more easily understood. Now, if it is true that if the gulf exists and that in a modern scientific and secular world we no longer have sympathy with or even comprehend the supernatural and transcendental language of our forebears, then the Christian religion becomes primarily a matter of morals. The goal is the achievement of justice and harmony in the social and political spheres and the living out of a high ideal of personal behaviour as exemplified in the life and death of Jesus of Nazareth. This makes the proposition of an incarnation, especially as it has been couched in the remote philosophical categories of the Chalcedonian definition, simply unnecessary. The postulating of a mysterious union between the natural realm and the supernatural at a single point in history can be seen for what it is—a metaphysical speculation at best, a logical absurdity at worst—and can be dismissed. Important consequences then follow: the outrageous claim of Christianity to be a unique revelation of the truth about human existence dissolves; the offensive authoritarian attitude of the Church can be disregarded; and the rites of initiation and communion can be reduced to the level of sociological and psychological necessity: pleasing symbols and rites, like those of freemasonry, by which group solidarity is expressed. About the existence of God, a power within and beyond this world, one is able to remain, at least provisionally, convinced. But as to the nature of this God one can be decently reticent, except to say that the power is not malevolent and that, somehow, in Jesus there has been a gleam of what it might be like to be in close contact with that power.

I am not trying to ridicule this position. The ideals are noble and have been around for at least two centuries of

Christian history. Many exponents, like Don Cupitt in his two most recent books, *Taking Leave of God* and *The Life of the World to Come*, argue that some such set of ideals is the only possible way of life for human beings living in the wake of the Enlightenment. I am merely asking whether this is adequate as an answer to the despairing question raised by man's terrified sense of being trapped, with no hope for the future. I am prepared to take seriously Dietriech Bonhoeffer's concept of man 'come of age', but I cannot accept, whatever may have happened to civilization as a result of that shift of thought and feeling which we call the Enlightenment, that there is a radical discontinuity with the past. The questions of Sophocles and Shakespeare seem as real to me as the questions of Brecht and Beckett. Nor, looking around me, do I find any assurance that it is possible for human beings, as Don Cupitt argues, 'to practise religion for its own sake' (even if they wanted to), and to practise it in such a way that faith having become 'internalized and moralized' we 'set out to attain a better world to come'. Would that it were possible. I can only see that our 'coming of age' has increased the anguish of our trapped existence. We are in the position of Caliban when he pitifully accuses Prospero of cruelty:

> You taught me language, and my profit on 't
> Is, I know how to curse: the red plague rid you
> For learning me your language!
> (The Tempest, Act i, Sc. 2)

All man's vast potential, the 'language' he has learned, has not taught him how to bless his world. If, to take one instance, the most obvious effect (and I am not denying other effects that may actually be beneficial) of gaining control over nuclear energy has been that a paralysing fear of destruction has been implanted in the heart of man, then the situation is, as Camus saw long before the atom was split, absurd. And it will remain absurd until there is the recognition that the language we have learned is the language of God, and that the only time it will turn into blessing in our mouths is when the creator of that language, the Divine Word, speaks in and through our flesh. That is why I have called the incarnation the foundation of hope.

I am quite sure that I shall be accused of trundling out on rusty wheels an ancient doctrine which, like those of nineteenth-century Liberal Protestantism, is equally irrelevant to modern conditions, and worse: of answering a question about absurdity with a proposition that is itself absurd. I believe I am doing neither of these things here. First, the mere fact that the incarnation is an ancient belief cannot preclude it from having fundamental significance for the modern world, though the ways in which the belief has been apprehended and expressed at different stages of the Church's history will, naturally, have been moulded by the contemporary needs and pressures of these stages and may well hold little of interest to those living in the twentieth century. In answer to the second accusation it could be said that, living as we do in a world where the hopes and promises of the Enlightenment have gone sour, to present an absurd resolution to an absurd set of circumstances has a certain slightly perverse attractiveness about it, at the level of game-playing. If we must all be absurd, and cannot be rational, then we may as well be religious as suicidal. Needless to say, that is not the way out of the dilemma, and I see no necessity for presenting the incarnation as an intrinsically absurd belief. It is a mysterious and supernatural event, to be sure, but that is not the same thing as saying it is absurd.

Several years ago I heard Professor John Taylor voicing a question which has always vexed the unbelieving mind: 'Why should there be something and not nothing?' It is probably the only question which the unbelieving scientist finds baffling; everything else seems within the reach of explanation, but this, the fact of being, is the first of all mysteries. For the Christian the question is no easier than for the scientist, but, given the fact of the creative activity of God, why he should have chosen to create is, intrinsically, a question no less absurd than why he should then have chosen to enter into his creation. An act of incarnation is certainly no more mysterious than an act of creation and, perhaps, less puzzling.

15

There is no reason, except on *a priori* philosophical grounds, that is because one assumes certain things about the nature of God, why the taking of human flesh should be regarded as incompatible with God's nature and activity.

A similar point has been made by Karl Stern in his autobiography *Pillar of Fire*. He recalls a meeting with Martin Buber in which the celebrated Jewish scholar was perplexedly pondering on the problem of what it was that Moses actually heard when the Lord addressed him on Mount Sinai.

> He began to talk of the giving of the law . . . and whether God really pronounced the ten commandments Himself in His own voice . . . He became quite pensive and said something to the effect that we do not know how to take this description of the miracle of Sinai, and whether the people actually *heard* God.

Stern, born and raised a Jew, became a Christian shortly afterwards and clearly sees this meeting with Buber and the conversation as having played some part in his conversion, for he goes straight on to make a point about the divinity of Christ. To suppose that God would really talk to human beings was no less incredible than to suppose he would become a human being: '. . . if that Voice was possible, then the Incarnation was possible too'. The miracles are not of a different order.

Perhaps 'miracle' is not the appropriate word to use in this context, except when describing the original creative act of God. Let us consider seriously an interpretation of the incarnation which has surfaced from time to time in the Church's history but will, undoubtedly, sound strange to modern ears. It is a view of the incarnation of the Son of God in Jesus Christ that does not see it as an extrinsic act, that is as something done to and for man by God, but as something inevitable and predestined: the true culmination of the original act of creation. In short, creation and incarnation are the two parts of a single action of God.

I have said that this interpretation of the incarnation will sound strange to ears that have grown accustomed to placing

16

the incarnation within the framework of the cross and the work of atonement. In Western Christianity this has normally been the framework, and it has helped to obscure the picture of God's action; but there have been thinkers who have tried to release the picture from its constricting surround.

If the name of the medieval theologian Duns Scotus (1264–1308) is known at all to modern Christians it is almost certainly connected with this understanding of the incarnation. The theory is that it was always God's will to become incarnate; that the flesh-taking of the Word of God was independent of the Fall of man; that the union of God with man in this way would have taken place even if there had been no Fall and no sin. The theory may be regarded as unconventional and speculative, but it is nowhere forbidden to Christian faith and it is not merely the brainchild of a singularly inventive medieval theologian. It can be found in Duns Scotus's contemporaries Albert the Great and Bonaventura, and later it is approached, tentatively, by Calvin. Thomas Aquinas was prepared to admit that it was possible to maintain that the incarnation was ordained from all times and would have occurred whether man had fallen or not, but he was unwilling, himself, to argue that such an interpretation was the most fitting understanding of God's action in the light of what he regarded had been revealed in Holy Scripture.

> . . . since everywhere in the Sacred Scriptures the sin of the first man is assigned as the reason of the Incarnation, it is more in accordance with this to say that the work of the Incarnation was ordained by God as a remedy for sin; so that, had sin not existed, the Incarnation would not have been. Although the power of God is not limited to this:— even had not sin existed, God could have become incarnate (*Summa Theologica* Pt. III, q.i. art. III).

More recently B. F. Westcott was a powerful advocate of this theory, as was Charles Williams. And still more recently Karl Rahner has recognized it as the implication of his own approach to the doctrines of God and man.

Westcott outlined his position as follows, in an essay of 1886 called 'The Gospel of Creation':

> ... it can fairly be maintained that we are led by Holy Scripture to regard the circumstances of the Incarnation as separable from the idea of Incarnation, and to hold that the circumstances of the Incarnation were due to sin, while the idea of the Incarnation was due to the primal and absolute purpose of love foreshadowed in Creation, apart from which sin was contingent.

The union of God and man in Christ is to be seen not as something added to the material universe, introduced, as it were, to correct a plan that had gone tragically wrong; on the contrary, this union is the culmination of the creative work of the Father. It follows from this that grace is not a kind of repair work performed on a damaged machine, nor a kind of spiritual tonic to provide individuals with the necessary energy for living their dying lives. It flows from the incarnation and is the self-communication of God to man in such a way that man actually shares the life of his creator. This is the purpose for which he was made. He possesses that 'supernatural existential' and can only be fulfilled supernaturally.

This reading of the incarnation, therefore, is no medieval speculation: something which we might find intellectually entertaining and which we can enjoyably consider as an interesting possibility; it seriously affects the way in which we think about God and the kind of hope we have for the destiny of man. If the incarnation is not understood as the purpose of creation then what I have called the 'divinization' of man, which I have already suggested is man's true end, looks a peculiar, and improbable, form of the rescue of man from decay and death.

The concept of divinization (*theosis*) has a long history in Christian doctrine and devotion and has remained, to this day, an essential strand of Eastern Orthodox theology. It stretches, in an explicit and extensive form, as far back as the fourth century to the writings of Gregory of Nyssa, but it is deeply embedded in nearly all of the thought of the early

18

Greek Fathers from the time of Irenaeus in the second century. So we are not introducing a novel concept into the Christian tradition, although our own understanding of divinization will, naturally, be conditioned by the circumstances of our own age. It is true that when the early Church spoke of the process of divinization which was begun in the incarnation of the Word of God (God became man in order that man might become divine), it often spoke from the categories of the Greek philosophical tradition with its basic assumption of a dichotomy between body and soul. The Fathers, therefore, frequently saw divinization as the soul's achievement of its desire for, and longing to share in, a spiritual, immaterial existence out of reach of the hampering clay of the body. But there is much more to the concept than can be contained in the terms of Greek philosophy, and we need not use the categories of body and soul at all. The supernatural destiny of man does not stand as a contradiction of man's natural existence; it is drawing of man in and through the natural existence and is the only conclusion of that existence. The future life of freedom in God does not come in the carefree abandonment of a physical shape which has chained the soul to the material world. What is involved here is the transformation of matter itself, an eschatological concept which sees the whole of creation caught up in the promise of God to man. Perhaps some such notion as this was already stirring in the mind of St Paul when he wrote to the Romans: '. . . the creation itself will be set free from its bondage to decay and obtain the glorious liberty of the children of God'.

That passage from the eighth chapter has always struck me as having a remarkably modern sound to it. There is in our world a preoccupation with the subject of freedom; the lack of it and the necessity for it are part of the consciousness of contemporary life. In our concept of divinization the Christian offers to the world the freedom of God. Only in the creator of the universe can absolute freedom be found: it is one of the attributes of God, and only God can liberate absolutely. Hans Urs von Balthasar has pointed out that God's free 'revelation of himself in Jesus Christ is an invitation into the realm of

19

absolute and divine freedom, in which alone human freedom can be fully realized' (*Engagement with God*, p. 19). If one asks the question, then, what can man's freedom 'in God' be like? the answer is found in the person of Jesus Christ who is the revealer and communicator of that freedom. Here in Christ is achieved the breakthrough and entry into that sphere that could not otherwise have been entered. Here in the realm of freedom inhabited and offered by the incarnate Lord is our peace. The freedom that is to be achieved is not merely the liberation from the powers of sin and evil—that would only be a negative kind of freedom—but a freedom which comes as part of the promise of creation: the incorporation of the world into the freedom of the life of God.

Again, I must suppose that this kind of language will sound strange to modern Christians. I doubt whether those who are regular worshippers have ever heard a sermon in which the hope of divinization has been seriously expounded by the preacher. Anglicans and Roman Catholics may well be familiar with the prayer which used to appear in the *Book of Common Prayer* (1928) as the collect for the second Sunday after Christmas, 'Almighty God, who didst wonderfully create man in thine own image, and didst yet more wonderfully restore him: Grant, we beseech thee, that as thy Son Our Lord Jesus Christ was made in the likeness of men, so we may be made partakers of thy divine nature . . .', and scarcely notice that it speaks about the salvation and final destiny of man precisely in terms of entering into and sharing the divine life. It is interesting to note in passing that the very next collect in the Prayer Book, that for the Feast of the Epiphany, speaks about salvation in similar terms: '. . . that we may have the fruition of thy glorious Godhead'. It is an astonishing phrase (though not strange to medieval theology or the Shorter Scottish Catechism), but one which has been made meaningless by the way in which modern English usage has altered the meaning of the word 'fruition' from 'enjoyment' to something like 'fruit'.

However, these two collects are comparatively rare instances of the liturgical expression of *theosis*, for the portrayal of redemption in this way never passed into the bloodstream of Western theology and devotion. (Even Augustine's famous statement, 'my heart is restless until it finds its rest in Thee', though full of yearning for God, is individualistic in tone and passive in conception.) Western Christianity, from the time of Augustine, has tended to view the incarnation through the spectacles of sin: the birth of the incarnate Word has become the remedy for sin and estrangement from God, a means by which God's justice and mercy could be reconciled. As man, whose guilt called for eternal punishment, could not pay the penalty for sin, God sent his own Son. 'There was no other good enough . . .' Hence, preachers of the gospel, even when they have been aware of how strong a strain in Christian thought the idea of divinization has been, are apprehensive about expounding it, and have avoided the theme for fear of sounding mystical or Pelagian. It is neither.

First, it is not 'mystical' in the strict sense of that word for it is not primarily concerned with freeing the individual soul of earthly limitations in order to experience a rapturous union with its transcendent creator. Though deeply concerned about the transformation of every human personality it is not individualistic, because it speaks both about the future of the whole of humanity and also about the future of the world in which humanity is located. Second, it is not Pelagian because it does not imply that man, however sublime his destiny, has in himself the power to transcend his limitations, free himself and achieve that sublimity. Had that been possible there would have been no need for the incorporation of manhood into Godhead in the incarnation, or the subsequent gift of the Holy Spirit. Further, it does not fail, as Pelagianism does, to recognize the seriousness of sin and the futility of life lived under the presence of evil. The kind of *theologia gloriae* which Luther feared is not being constructed in this interpretation of the incarnation. It is true that we start with the idea of glory, seen as the end of man, and read all events in the light of that end, but the cross of Christ is an integral part of the pattern of that glory. The *theologia gloriae* incorporates the *theologia crucis*.

21

The fourth evangelist dramatically demonstrates such an 'incorporation' in the passion and resurrection narratives of his Gospel. Here the two 'theologies' interpenetrate each other at every point; and the most compelling instance of all occurs in the description of the appearance of the risen Lord to Thomas. The evangelist has already told us that Thomas was not with the disciples on the occasion of the first resurrection appearance, and Thomas, doubting the veracity of the reports, demands to handle the glorious scars. Eight days later he is invited to do just that: the risen body carries the ineradicable marks of human sin and death. The devotion to the wounds of Christ in Catholic tradition is not, or should not be, the sign of a morbid sentimentality which focuses upon physical suffering; it is a sign of the serene recognition that pain and death are transformed by the power of God; that the pattern of glory which is the life of God is one which takes into itself the worst horrors of man's existence. 'God becomes man', Hans Urs von Balthasar writes, 'in order that man may not be left with any anti-divine experience that God himself had not undergone . . . it is necessary that all cosmic forces should be disarmed by God himself' (*Engagement with God*, p. 37).

So when we eliminate the causal connection between the sin of man and the incarnation of the Word we are not pushing the cross of Christ to an insignificant edge of the picture, we are placing it in its proper perspective as part of a scene which stretches from creation through incarnation to divinization. When we agree with Westcott about the 'absolute purpose of love foreshadowed in Creation, apart from which sin was contingent', we are saying that sin was a fact which God had to take into account as he unfolded the plan of his love. Man is 'fallen' and the conditions brought about by the 'Fall' become the inescapable circumstances of the incarnate life. All the consequences of original sin—the alienation from God, the disintegration of human society and the human personality, the sense of utter helplessness and ultimate loss, the experience of death itself—had to be endured by the incarnate Lord. Because of sin, the divinization of man

22

has to be accomplished in this manner, that is by death and resurrection, and no other.

I have spoken of the dilemma of modern man: of the experience of an apparently irreconcilable contradiction at the heart of human existence; and I have tried to indicate that the incarnation offers the only resolution of this contradiction. When J. H. Newman wrote his *Essay in Aid of a Grammar of Assent* he faced the same problem and offered the same solution in a remarkable and characteristically intricately textured sentence. 'Christ', he wrote, reconciles 'conflicting and diverging descriptions by embodying them in one common representative'. I have called these 'conflicting descriptions' the experience of contradiction, and I see, too, the embodiment of the reconciliation of the contradiction in Christ. It is only when both the degradation of God is seen in the cross and the glory of man is seen in the resurrection and ascension that the terrible dilemma of man's existence can be seen to be resolved, for man's contradictory awareness of his capacity for self-transcendence and his utter helplessness can only be resolved in the place where the limitlessness of God's being co-inheres with the limitedness of man's being. That is why I have called the incarnation the foundation of hope. The life, death and resurrection of Jesus Christ are not only the pledge of the renewal of the world, but also the actual cause of the renewal. In the person of Christ the exchange of life for life is made; in him God is human and man is divine; the life is a historical fact: the exchange is an eternal reality.

Chapter 2

THE WORLD OF POLITICS

From the beginning the problem of the relationship between religion and politics has troubled Christianity. Was the kingdom of God to be understood as a personal, inward, spiritual possession, or was it, perhaps, a supernatural, even apocalyptic concept? Did its proclamation entail more than a change to the ways in which individuals lived their lives and include the making of changes to the structures of society? The paradoxical command to Christians to be 'in the world' but not 'of the world' offered widely different interpretations of the degree of Christian involvement in social and political institutions. The problem surfaced as early as the earliest documents of the Bible, and we find both Peter and Paul giving a prominent place in their moral teaching to the question of the proper attitudes the followers of Christ ought to adopt to those who exercised political authority over them. When the expected Parousia did not occur and the Church grew and spread to the farthest reaches of the Roman Empire, the issue, inevitably, deepened and broadened to embrace not only the issue of individual behaviour, but also that of the whole body of believers to the state. My task here is not to survey the complicated history of Church and state relations, but to examine the truth or falsity of the claim that 'the Christian dream of a city of God has lost all serious content in the modern world' (so wrote Frederic Raphael in a recent article in the *New York Herald Tribune*). It is also to assess the adequacy of the notion that 'the pulpit is no place for politics' because 'the Church's first duty is to nurture individual Christians' (so wrote Peregrine Worsthorne in a recent article in the *Sunday Telegraph*). And I must perform this task in the light of what I have already said about the incarnation as the foundation for Christian hope and action. If the incarnation is indeed the doctrine upon which all other doctrines are built, in what way will it shape our attitude to the perplexing question of the relationship between politics and religion? Does belief in the incarnation mean that the gospel is individual or social? And if social, should actual systems of government be subject to theological assessment?

I have already referred to Karl Marx and, indeed, have used one of his phrases as the title for this book, and so I turn to him again now; for when he surveyed the social and political conditions of Western Europe in 1848 and produced the *Communist Manifesto* he clearly believed that 'the Christian dream of a city of God' had long lost all serious content and should be exposed for the fraud it was. Four years earlier, in an essay with the cumbersome title *Towards a Critique of Hegel's Philosophy of Right, Introduction*, he had spoken directly about the evaporating dream as humanity gradually awakened out of its sleep. 'Man has found in the imaginary reality of heaven where he looked for a superman only the reflection of his own self' (*Selected Writings*, p. 63). His argument is well known: the achievement of reality and freedom would need the destruction of religious institutions. Religion was illusory, and with its beautiful dreams it had provided seductive consolations for the enslaved members of the human race. Its destruction would be painful—it would rob man of a kind of comfort— but it was necessary. 'Religious suffering is at the same time an expression of real suffering and a protest against real suffering. Religion is the sigh of the oppressed creature, the feeling of a heartless world, and the soul of soulless circumstances. It is the opium of the people' (p. 64).

This famous passage is a more vivid and epigrammatic statement of a point he had made earlier in his highly significant review of two articles by his contemporary, Bruno Bauer, on the Jewish question. In arguing for the emancipation of the Jews, Bauer had proposed the disestablishment of the Christian Church and the 'dissolution' of Christianity. 'If

26

they wish to become free, the Jews should not profess Christianity, but the dissolution of Christianity, the general dissolution of religion, i.e. the Enlightenment, criticism and its result, free humanity' (p. 57). Marx takes up the argument: it is social ills that give rise to religious beliefs, and disestablishment will do nothing to affect those ills. He sees all men, not only Jews, in need of emancipation: '. . . since the existence of religion is the existence of a defect, the source of this defect can only be sought in the nature of the state itself. . . . We do not change secular questions into theological ones. We change theological questions into secular ones' (p. 44). In this same essay he sees right into the heart of the Christian's perplexity about the relationship between politics and religion when he asserts: 'In its own consciousness the Christian state is an ideal whose realization is unattainable.'

I have chosen to start with Karl Marx's words for three reasons. First, because the rapidity with which Marxism has overtaken the political systems of more than a third of the population of the globe is so extraordinary a historical phenomenon that it cannot be ignored in any discussion of religion and politics. Second, because Marx took religion seriously: he realized that any attempt at freeing the people by revolutionizing the structures of society would have to take into serious account the extent of the power exercised by religion over the hearts and minds of its adherents. It could not be left to wither and die by itself; and the unrelenting hostility usually shown by Communist regimes to religion of all kinds is the practical consequence of Marx's own attitude. Third, and perhaps most importantly, we have in Karl Marx the most influential philosopher of the last hundred years and, as in the case of Albert Camus, one of the most eloquent critics of the Church. It is in the face of this challenge that the Church must act and offer its own conception of the world that is to be gained.

I have already remarked that only the Hebrew-Christian intellectual tradition could have produced the thought of Marx, and I must go on to observe that there is much in his critique of society that Christianity should recognize as true

27

and welcome with gratitude. What he observed in nineteenth-century industrial Europe was a society in which the majority of the population was exploited and oppressed, and that at the centre of this unhappiness was the condition of 'alienation'. Because of the capitalist system workers were alienated from that for which they worked: the product of their labour. The system was constructed like a machine, and the men working the machine were expendable pieces of that machine. Production was controlled not by those actually doing the work but by those who had the money to own the machine. Thus, Marx argued, men, alienated as they were from their work, were dehumanized; each man imprisoned in his own cell as the whole of the proletariat was imprisoned in a system which separated money from labour and saw increasing production as the goal of human achievement. This pitiful and intolerable situation could be endured by those who suffered because of the dreams provided by religion, 'the opium of the people'. What could not be attained in this life— freedom, fulfilment, happiness—was promised for a life to come; and the Protestant Churches with their traditional emphasis upon the necessity for the individual to be obedient to the state seemed to Marx to buttress the capitalist system and tighten the chains of an already enslaved people. The state itself was the actual means by which the proletariat was dominated. 'Political power . . . is merely the organized power of one class for oppressing another. . . . The executive of the modern state is but a committee for managing the affairs of the whole bourgeoisie' (p. 60). For Marx the only solution was the destruction of the entire system; in short, the revolution of the proletariat and the abolition of the state, for, however that state was structured, so long as the capitalist system remained the state would ineluctably operate as an integral part of the process of alienation.

Marx was a philosopher: he analysed the situation, diagnosed the ills and laid the intellectual foundations for a radical change in human affairs, but he gave no detailed, practical guidance as to how this change was to be effected, and in the century following his death we have seen, in the varying

attempts to create communist societies, hugely differing interpretations of what Marx intended. Many of them have
been as oppressive (though, of course, in different ways) as
any political system which Marx himself had experienced in
nineteenth-century Europe.

It is tempting for a liberal democrat to survey the political
history of Eastern Europe since 1945 and claim that Marxism
inevitably leads in directions which would have dismayed its
founder: the growth of bureaucracy, the increase of the power
of the state, the suppression of individual freedom. The evidence seems to be there, but Marxism is relatively young as
a kind of political system and the 'evidence' only counts for
something if one can see that the foundations of Communism,
the political philosophy of Marx, whatever its virtues, is fun-
damentally misguided. One would argue that the noble in-
tentions of the philosopher could never be realized in the
ways he imagined because of a fundamental misconception
about the nature of the creature he was supposed to be setting
free.

Nearly all Christian critiques of Marxism have attacked it
at its most obviously vulnerable point: its optimistic assessment of human nature (which has now revealed itself to us
as a typically nineteenth-century attitude). The reason why
the Church has been sceptical about all forms of utopianism
is not so much that it has had its eyes so fixed on heaven that
it could not see earth as that it is doubtful about the capacity
of human beings to live together in perfect harmony. The
doctrine of original sin is simply the description of a state of
affairs in which destruction and unhappiness are caused not
by weakness or failure but by the wilful self-seeking of each
individual human heart. It seemed as though Marx was incapable of even entertaining the possibility that the oppression of one person by another, or of one group by another,
was not merely a stage in the development of the human race,
but actually a symptom of a universal human malaise; that
it was the 'sin' which produced the system and not the system
which produced the sin. It should be remarked that it is not
surprising that Marx should have conceived his philosophy

29

in this way. How could he not be affected by the intellectual excitement of the progress in the natural sciences, by ideas of evolution and, especially, by the new discoveries about the importance of the relationship of a species to its environment? In this climate he claimed that he had founded a new science of economics, though, as David McLellan has indicated, the word *Wissenschaft* has wider implications in German than its equivalent, 'science', in English. Nevertheless, the influences of the sciences are clearly there, and his dream of a future in which man would finally be free was one which he believed could be realized by the radical alteration of the economic and political environment of that spieces, man.

To argue, on the basis of a belief in the doctrine of original sin, against the utopian dream of Karl Marx, need not drive us into the embrace of Thomas Hobbes, whose view of human nature was so low that he became an advocate of a kind of political absolutism that almost went as far as conscious oppression. Nor does it leave us in a position of cynical detachment, prepared to accept the *status quo*, any *status quo*—democratic, autocratic, communist—on the grounds that human beings, unregenerate as they are, will remain essentially unaffected by their economic and social conditions.

I have said that there is in Marx's critique of society much that the Church should recognize as true and receive with gratitude. Few of its own spokesmen in the nineteenth century denounced the dehumanizing conditions of millions of working people with as much force as he did; or even saw them with as much clarity. His passionate desire for the freedom and self-fulfilment of all members of society should only have been welcomed by a Church which had preserved the story of its Lord reading from the prophecy of Isaiah: 'He has sent me to proclaim release to the captives and recovery of sight to the blind, to set at liberty those who are oppressed', and his comment, 'Today this scripture has been fulfilled in your hearing' (Luke 4:18 ff). Of even greater importance was his stress on the fact that human existence is a political problem as well as an individual one. Throughout his writings there is a stress on that aspect of existence which the Churches of

30

Protestant Europe, in particular, had tended to ignore: the corporate nature of human life and the solidarity and interdependence of all members of the human race. It is sometimes said that Marxism, like all totalitarian regimes, destroys personal freedom by elevating the needs of society above those of the individual, but there is no sign of this in the early writings of Marx. Here we find the conviction that 'society' and 'individual' are inseparable and complementary concepts; the relationship between them is symbiotic, though the individual can only find fulfilment in society.

In an essay called *The Relationship of the Church and the World in the Light of a Political Theology*, J. B. Metz indicates the way in which that movement of thought and feeling which spread across Europe in the seventeenth and eighteenth centuries, and which we call the Enlightenment, finally dismantled the attempted medieval synthesis of religion and politics, of Christianity and culture. What can be traced in European history is the growth of the concept of the 'individual' and the increasing value placed upon 'individuality', and what is achieved in the period of the Enlightenment (and demonstrated philosophically in Rationalism and Idealism) is the culmination of this process: the absolute autonomy of the individual. Religion became increasingly personal and interiorized. Faith was no longer a communal matter to be practised in public but a matter of private decision and commitment. The problem of the Christian's political activity now becomes acute because there is a radical separation between the individual and the *polis*. Charity, for example, becomes the exercise of 'a private virtue with no political relevance; it is a matter of the I–Though relation' (p. 257). The category of personal encounter becomes predominant; even the Bible is to be read as God's self-communication to individual hearts and minds, while the Church exists solely to nurture the spiritual lives of individual believers. At the level of secular thinking this growth of the belief in the autonomy of the individual led, eventually, to the sense, already finding expression in the latter years of the nineteenth century, of the utter isolation of the individual and to the sense of despair and absurdity which has characterized the various kinds of Existentialist philosophy in this century.

Marx's philosophy stands in sharp contrast to the folly and danger of this excessive individualism: he would not see society in other than organic terms, and therefore could only see the possibility of changing the lives of individuals in the overturning of the whole structure of society.

It is only comparatively recently that the Church, perhaps shocked into a reassessment of itself by the sudden spread of Marxism, has looked into the source of the power of that philosophy and has begun to rediscover and find new meanings in those metaphors which have been used in Scripture and the liturgy to describe the ideal state of human existence: the city, the kingdom, the body, Adam. In the wake of this recovery of the sense of the importance of the notion of human solidarity a 'theology of liberation' has grown. It is a theology which insists that the promise of salvation is not merely a matter of individual concern to be faced and worked out in a private encounter between the saviour and the saved, but is also a communal and 'public' matter. It insists that the eschatological promises of God—justice, liberty, reconciliation, peace—are not only vague dreams of hope held out to discrete individuals who have kept the faith, blissful conditions in a land called heaven, but possible conditions for which Christians should be fighting here and now. So, where there is injustice and oppression, the changing of society by revolution is considered. 'If love is actualized as the unconditional determination to freedom and justice for others, there might be circumstances where love itself could demand actions of a revolutionary character' (p. 266).

One of the most lucid accounts of the way the political dilemma affects the Christian conscience has come not from the pen of any Liberation theologian of Latin America, but from that of Graham Greene in his novel *The Honorary Consul*. In 1973 he published this story of the attempted kidnapping of an honorary British consul in Argentina by a small band of Paraguayan revolutionaries under the leadership of an unfrocked priest, Leon Rivas. He is the focal point for the two major themes of the novel: the relationship between Church and state and the political responsibility of the individual Christian. This figure, a bundle of psychological and emotional contradictions, is a dramatic embodiment of the several conflicting strains running through contemporary Christian thinking about politics. At one point he tries to defend his violent actions by expatiating on the scriptural text, 'Render unto Caesar the things that are Caesar's':

> 'Christ was a man,' Fr. Rivas said, 'even if some of us believe that he was God as well. It was not God the Romans killed, but a man. A man who lived in his own province, in his own particular way. He had no idea of the kind of world we would be living in now. Render unto Caesar, but when *our* Caesar uses napalm and fragmentation bombs . . . I think perhaps the memory of that man, that carpenter, can lift a few people out of the temporary Church of these terrible years, when the Archbishop sits down to dinner with the General, into the great Church beyond our time and place' (p. 275).

Rivas clearly understands the words of Christ to be an order to submission and refuses to accept that order for the oppressed people of Latin America. In his violent, revolutionary actions he takes forward the arguments of much Liberation theology that has appeared in Latin America in the last few decades: it is not only individual generals and archbishops who are greedy, corrupt, weak, or simply wrong, but the political system which permits such connivance of Church and state.

This theology may be wrong when, and if, it sees in Marxism a way of breaking down the oppressive regimes and constructing free and open societies; for the 'ultimate command to love' stands equally as a judgement on a communist society which sees the suppression of individual freedoms as a necessary stage in the struggle to achieve the freedom of a group as it does on a capitalist society which considers human beings as a means of production. But it surely cannot be wrong in its effort to recover the idea and the actuality of the true *polis*, and to show the world that 'the Christian dream of the city of God' has not lost all serious content.

But what will be this content? What kind of city can we expect to be built? Once one has recovered the knowledge of the mutual interdependence of all human lives and the awareness that politics cannot be something apart from individual Christian life and practice, will one assume that the Church and the state are identical, or should have the same boundaries, and try to build or rebuild Christendom? Will there be, as in Oliver Cromwell's England or seventeenth-century New England, the promulgation of specifically, or even exclusively, Christian laws? Can one build the kingdom of God on earth? Is the state the anticipation of the heavenly city? The theocracies of the past, even those which accomplished great things—Israel, Byzantium, Geneva—pass before our eyes as examples of political failure. And Marx's 'classless society', supposing that society could be Christian, does not hold out the hope of the perfect content for the Christian dream. So today 'Christian spokesmen may proclaim their secularity as much as they please. It is quite another matter to suppose that the saeculum will ever again call itself Christian' (S. Crites, p. 17).

To say that does not, however, force us to leave 'the dream' without content and Karl Marx unanswered. But we must be wary of trying to deduce the content directly from the teachings of Jesus. One of the most important achievements of biblical scholarship during the last century and a half has been to release us from the simplistic conviction that it is possible to find the kind of systematic moral philosophy in the teachings of the Lord from which all social and political programmes could be logically drawn. We cannot deduce what we should actually do about the poor by following the teachings of the Sermon on the Mount, or how we should treat the sick by contemplating the healing miracles. Furthermore, almost every one of Jesus's recorded utterances which had any political reference is enigmatic. The account, for instance, of the confrontation between Pilate and Jesus in the eighteenth chapter of the fourth Gospel is a masterly

34

example of theological and dramatic irony. The answers of Jesus to Pilate's straightforward questions leave Pilate in doubt about the terms he has used. 'Kingdom' and 'world' are not simply contrasting concepts; supernatural and natural connotations merge into one another in a way that leaves Pilate, and anyone looking for a plain answer, bewildered. And even the famous question, 'Is it lawful to pay taxes to Caesar, or not?' (Mark 12:14), is teasingly set aside by Jesus with a reply which can be read neither as a proof-text for the absolute separation of life into two spheres, sacred and secular, nor as a command to his followers to refrain from involvement in the affairs of state. Instead, it is a baffling answer which throws the question back into the laps of those who have asked it with the intention of forcing them into a decision about the status of his own person. It is, certainly, impossible from such ambiguous utterances to trace the definite views of Peter and Paul back to any known words of Jesus.

Such content as we are likely to give it is to be drawn, therefore, not directly out of the teachings of Jesus, but out of the implications of God's involvement with the world in what we call the incarnation. If the Son of God has united himself to his Father's creation in this manner, there can be no part of human life which is incapable of sanctification; and because politics, the life of the 'city', is essentially the matter of ordering the relationships between individuals in community, then the proper ordering of those relationships can never be a matter that has no relevance for Christians. 'The Christian's involvement [in the world] has its origins in God's involvement for the sake of the world; it is grounded in it, captivated by it, shaped and directed by it' (Balthasar, *Engagement with God*, p. 67).

First, Christianity is forbidden to develop a 'pariah' mentality. The temptation to do just that has always been there, and there are signs that the earliest Christians frequently saw themselves in this light. Abolished from the synagogues of the Jews, despised by the pagans, they knew themselves to be the outcasts of the world as they clung to a faith that was both puzzling and contemptible to the rest of humanity. So, Paul in his first letter to the Corinthians writes as a 'pariah': 'We have become, and are now, as the refuse of the world, the offscouring of all things' (1 Cor. 4:13). The books both of the New Testament and of the Apocrypha are full of indications that there were elements in the early Church which advocated and practised as much withdrawal from the world as possible. 'Do not love the world or the things in the world. If any one loves the world, love for the Father is not in him' (1 John 2:15). Those elements remain to this day, and perhaps are stronger than they have been for centuries. The mentality of the 'pariah' can be observed not only in 'exclusive' sects, but in both the Catholic and the Protestant traditions. (I am not now referring to monasticism: that is an entirely different phenomenon with a different psychological basis.) What has been growing up in Western Christianity is a movement which, impatient with, and frustrated by, the structures of the Church and fearful of the encroachment of secularism and liberalism, encourages small groupings of Christians who share an intimate kind of fellowship which is based upon the knowledge that they are separated by their faith from the rest of society.

Hannah Arendt, in an illuminating study, *On Humanity in Dark Times*, has pointed out how much there is to be gained, psychologically and emotionally, from belonging to a 'pariah' group. The times we live in are, perhaps, even darker than when she wrote the essay, and when there is violence and fear abroad individuals seek small groups in which they can find comfort and security. This, until recently, has been the case of the world's great persecuted race, the Jews, and Arendt describes how a 'pariah' group generates a 'warmth of human relationships which may strike those who have had experience of such groups as an almost physical phenomenon' (p. 21). These words could have been a description of almost any of the newly formed charismatic groups of the modern Christian scene. A price has been paid for this warmth of course: homelessness or worldlessness. 'But we must not forget that the charm and intensity of the atmosphere that develops is also due to the fact that the pariahs of this world enjoy the great

36

privilege of being unburdened by care for the world.' This is the privilege which the Christian is denied, however much he may long for the peculiar warmth and security of the 'pariah' circle. God's involvement with the world in Christ places upon every Christian the burden of care for the world at all its interstices—including politics.

The Christian's place in society is not merely as an intelligent creature made by God with the freedom to shape the earth and the responsibility of building the world which he has been given, but as the lively embodiment of God's saving love for mankind. His task is the purification and redemption of those structures which determine the ordering of human relationships with the end of revealing to human beings their supernatural destiny. It is because the destiny is supernatural that the Christian acknowledges that the kingdom of God in its completeness can never be built on earth, that the saeculum can never be fully Christian, and so is able not to be downcast when human efforts at constructing the just and peaceful city fail. But that does not mean that the movement towards the achievement can be postponed until the after-life or interiorized into a private process. Nor can the goal be something looked forward to, and worked for, outside the political structures of any society—like the goal of the Jewish people. The Christian goal is not the restoration of a chosen people, it is the transformation of the world. The supernatural does not contradict the natural; it is that towards which the natural strives. The city of God cannot be built without the stones of natural society, so the Christian will, therefore, be an agent of change in society as a whole. In his identification with all those who suffer he will effect that change not only through private acts of charity but, where necessary, in open acts of opposition to societies whose structures easily admit the greedy accumulation of wealth and the oppression of the weak by the use of force. It is, therefore, right that the Church should have, and voice, views on, for example, the poverty of countries in Africa and Latin America, or the use of nuclear power.

When we return to our theological foundation we find that

in the incarnation we have the direct communication of the life of God to his world. That life is, moreover, revealed as the free and ceaseless exchange of love between the persons of the Holy Trinity, and it follows that the free exchange of love between human beings, made in the image of their creator, will be the life-blood of the body of mankind. Any system of government which prevents, through greed or callousness, the possibility of such free exchange must be criticized and condemned as contrary to the will of God. Any system which prevents the possibility of individual self-fulfilment must similarly be criticized and condemned, for self-fulfilment can only be found in the free exchange by human beings of love for one another and God. Grace—the movement of love from God to man—and worship—the movement of love from man to God—are the beginning and the end of human existence.

We may, finally, return to Karl Marx for he also believed in self-fulfilment, but it is on this last matter that the Marxist and the Christian part company with no hope of reconciliation. If Marx failed to recognize the tragedy of the human condition by his optimistic belief in the innate goodness of human nature, he failed also to recognize the glory of human nature with its supernatural potential. The world he hoped man would gain when the revolution had done its work is too domestic for the yearning, searching human spirit. When it came to envisaging that new world he could only say that the development of human energy was an end in itself and 'the true realm of freedom' (vol. 3, p. 68). So Hans Urs von Balthasar writes, with all such utopian philosophies as Marxism in mind: '. . . even the hope that in the perspective of world history, the world in years to come will be a "better world" than it was in the past, is from a Christian point of view at best a secondary kind of hoping . . .' (*Engagement with God*, p. 61). The destiny all utopian philosophies envisage falls far short of that transcendental destiny which is the substance of the Christian vision of the end of man.

Chapter 3

THE WORLD OF NATURE

Therefore am I still
A lover of the meadows and the woods,
And mountains; and of all that we behold
From this green earth; of all the mighty world
Of eye, and ear,—both what they half create,
And what perceive; well pleased to recognise
In nature and the language of the sense
The anchor of my purest thought, the nurse,
The guide, the guardian of my heart, and soul
Of all my moral being.

When William Wordsworth wrote those lines composed above
Tintern Abbey in 1798, the smoke was already beginning to
rise into the air above the new towns and industrial waste
from new factories already pouring into streams and rivers:
the Industrial Revolution was already far advanced. It is not
surprising that, for all its celebration of the countryside, there
is an unease in Wordsworth's poetry, almost a premonitory
sense of disaster. The consolation and reassurance the poet
sought in nature were the consolation and reassurance of the
power and harmony of the divine Mind. In a spirit of exal-
tation and peace he felt that in the natural world he could
'see into the life of things'. One wonders what kind of 'life' he
would see if he could peer into the rivers and lakes of
twentieth-century Europe and North America with their pol-
luted waters and their dead fish, or if he could look upon the
devastated forests of Brazil. What evidence of the providence
or majesty of God could such sights afford? The sense of

unease that we find not only in Wordsworth but in many of the Romantic poets is interesting: it does not arise out of opposition to scientific and technological progress as such—they were not Luddites—but out of a deep feeling that something was going seriously wrong with the human race and its environment; that man and nature had grown and were still growing apart. There can be no one alive now, one hundred and thirty years after Wordsworth's death, who, having given some thought to these matters, can be unaware of how seriously the relationship between man and nature has gone wrong.

With the publication of Rachel Carson's book *Silent Spring* twenty years ago the facts about the effects of man's treatment of his natural environment were at last brought to the notice of ordinary people. This was a serious, well-documented scientific study which could be understood by those who were not trained in the natural sciences, and for the first time it became generally known that the preservation of the ecology of the earth was a matter of deep concern. She dedicated the book to Albert Schweitzer, using some of his own words as a minatory epigraph: 'Man has lost the capacity to foresee and forestall. He will end by destroying the earth.' Her main purpose in *Silent Spring* was to show how the use of chemicals developed during and after the Second World War in the control of 'pests' were, in fact, destroying the earth by eliminating plant, insect and bird life as well as the pests, and were polluting water in lakes and rivers. She saw this poisoning of the environment, 'along with the possibility of the extinction of mankind by nuclear war', as 'the central problem of our age' (p. 8).

So powerful was her case that there have grown up in the last twenty years highly organized groups, and even political parties, which have taken her at her word and argue that the preservation of the natural world is the most important issue of contemporary life; and these have had some small impact on the way in which the industrial nations of Western civilization think and behave. Rachel Carson herself, in 1962, held out the hope that man was at last beginning to foresee and forestall, '. . . as it has become apparent that the heedless and unrestrained use of chemicals is a greater menace to ourselves than to the targets, the river which is the science of biotic control flows again fed by new streams of thought' (p. 279). But even as we have become more aware of our contamination of the environment, so our capacity for contaminating it has grown, and the difficulty of controlling the process of contamination has increased. Almost every day brings to light a new demonstration of the appalling consequences of our failure (deliberate or accidental) to harness the technological forces of our industrial society. For example, both *The Times* and *The Observer* newspapers in the first two weeks in June 1982 carried reports about 'acid rain': the collection in the atmosphere of clouds of destructive chemicals which could be carried by wind from the areas in which they were produced to parts of the world hundred of miles away, where they descended like weapons of war on another country's forests, rivers and lakes. *The Observer* reported on Sunday, 13 June:

> A confidential meeting of leading scientists and officials at the Department of the Environment on Friday appears to have agreed that by the end of the century acid rain may cause British uplands to suffer in a way that has already happened in Scandinavia where thousands of lakes are dead or dying as a result of pollution.

If a Christian is to speak seriously about the renewal of the world, then the matter of man's relationship to nature is not something which can be thought to be of secondary importance; it is as vital a question as the renewal of himself as an individual and the renewal of his relationships with others in society. It is as vital, moreover, because it is, or should be, inconceivable for the Christian to separate himself from the material world (nature) in such a way that its destruction or preservation is irrelevant to God's total action of salvation in Jesus Christ. If we have noticed that many Christians see no necessary connection between the incarnation and politics, we will notice that even more fail to see any connection between the activity of God in Christ and the activity of men

41

in nature. What, they will ask, have salvation and ecology to do with one another?

Before I try to draw out the implications of belief in the incarnation for our attitude towards our natural environment, a point needs to be made about the fundamental difference between the Christian attitude to survival and the secular. The sheer matter of 'survival' is, or should be, of little consequence to Christians. The Christian does not believe, first, that matter is eternal or, second, that this world and this life are all that there is. It has become part of scientific lore since the time of Charles Darwin's *Origin of Species* that the concept of survival is of crucial importance for the understanding of the evolutionary process; and it is true from personal experience that the instinct to survive seems to be among the most deeply implanted of all the instincts. The efforts of thousands of people to build shelters in the event of a nuclear war is also evidence of the lengths to which people will go in order to survive—regardless of the kind of world in which they would have to live as survivors of such a war. There is the common assumption that the human race must, at all costs, be preserved, must propagate, must survive *as a species*. The Darwinian zoologist will see this as a natural and necessary object: the Christian does not see it as natural and necessary at all. In saying this I am not, for a moment, contesting Darwin's theory of evolution as the 'survival of the fittest'; it may still be the best explanation of how the human species developed. I am, however, saying that the 'coming-to-consciousness' of man indicates that human existence is of far greater complexity than a cycle of 'birth, copulation and death'—eating, sleeping, fighting and surviving—would suggest. This 'coming-to-consciousness' has made man, as Julian Huxley frequently reminded us, the only species with some control over its own development, and capable of directing its progress towards its chosen destiny.

The whole force of the Christian gospel lies in its refusal to take survival as the *raison d'être* of the human personality, and in its paradoxical assertion that to lose one's life is to gain it. The cross is to be taken as the sign of victory, so the

42

'natural' instinct to survive is transformed by a supernatural willingness to abandon oneself in the action of a sacrificial love. It should not be a matter of great importance, therefore, to the Christian whether human life comes to an end or not; what is of importance is how that life is lived while it still exists. Furthermore, as I have said, the material world is not eternal: it came into being by the grace of God (however that origin is envisaged) and it has its destiny, its true end, with the human race in the life of its creator. This being so, the way in which humanity and matter 'fit together' is, similarly, of great importance.

The roots of our misuse of the earth's bounty, the wastage of food and power, as well as the destruction of the environment, have sometimes been traced back to the Hebrew-Christian doctrine of creation. In the book of Genesis's first account of creation God speaks to the human creature he has made: 'Be fruitful and multiply, and fill the earth and subdue it; and have dominion over the fish of the sea and over the birds of the air and over every living thing that moves upon the face of the earth.' From this divine command, it is argued, there developed in the Hebrew-Christian tradition an attitude towards the natural world that was rapacious and arrogant. The world had been made for man to use at his pleasure and he proceeded to subjugate it in the belief that this was the will of God. In fact this is a perversion of the tradition, and one wonders if those who make the accusation have read further in the Old Testament than this first chapter of Genesis. The second account of creation makes no mention of any dominion being given to man. It emphasizes instead his frail and 'clayey' nature.

Throughout the Old Testament the natural world is described as the theatre of God's glory: winds and seas, hills and plains, plants and animals are all signs of the beauty and majesty of God—not objects to be manipulated by man.

> Praise the Lord from the earth,
> you sea monsters and all deeps,

fire and hail, snow and frost,
      stormy wind fulfilling his command
                                      (Ps. 148).

  O let the earth bless the Lord: yea let it praise
    him and magnify him for ever.
  O ye mountains and hills bless the Lord . . . O all ye
    green things upon the earth bless the Lord
                  (*The Song of the Three Children*, Daniel ch. 3).

The creation exists in its loveliness and grandeur to bless its
creator; and in the 104th psalm an ideal picture of man living
and working in harmony with nature is painted:

    Thou dost cause the grass to grow for the cattle,
        and plants for man to cultivate,
    that he may bring forth food from the earth,
        and wine to gladden the heart of man.

There is nothing in the ancient Hebrew tradition to support
the claim that the command of God that man should subdue
the earth was construed as permission for the human race to
beat it into submission and thoughtlessly drain its resources.
  However, it is true that science and technology, the explor-
ation and consequent exploitation of the natural world, are
a growth out of the biblical doctrine of creation. The world,
freely created by God, is created quite distinct from God, and
man occupies a special place in that creation. In Judaism, as
later in Christianity and Islam, man is the inhabitant of two
worlds: 'then the Lord God formed man out of dust from the
ground, and breathed into his nostrils the breath of life; and
man became a living being' (Gen. 2:7). He is the pinnacle of
the natural order, the climax of God's creative activity, and
is also set apart from that natural order, 'So God created
man in his own image' (1:27). Had there been no conception
of the distinct reality of the world and man's singular place
in it, the world might still be believed to be in the thrall of
the demonic. Inhabited by spirits, gods or devils (Pan), nature
would certainly have been approached with reverence and

44

awe, but it could never have been subject to investigation and analysis.

It is true, too, that the Christian tradition developed the concept of the importance of man in the universe, but there is no classical formulation of creation which suggests that nature is simply an 'object' for man's pleasure, and that he has absolute power over it. If, for example, we turn to Thomas Aquinas, whose exposition of Christianity dominated the thought of Western Christendom for seven hundred years, we do, indeed, find him speaking about animals being subject to man: '. . . as the plants make use of the earth for their nourishment, and animals make use of plants . . . man makes use of both plants and animals' (*Summa Theologica*, Pt. 1 q. xcvi, 1). But we should be wrong if we interpreted this as the beginning of the modern 'objectification' of the environment. The idea of the divine *order*, almost a hierarchy of things in the universe, is central to Thomas Aquinas's understanding of creation. Each thing in the universe occupies its proper place and exists to serve those things which are ranged above it. In turn, each thing is given the capacity to use, but not to abuse, those things placed below it. The proper function of every particle of the created order is ordained by God. On grounds of Thomistic theology alone one could argue that the use to which man has put the world in which he lives and has responsibilities is a disruption of God's beneficent ordering of nature. The waste of natural resources or the destruction of animal and plant life for personal gain (the increase of power or wealth) is to upset what a later, and less religious, age would call 'the balance of nature'. Everything that existed, from the inanimate matter of sand and rock to the highest spiritual creatures, the seraphim and cherubim, were part of a single coherent whole: a chain of being of which the weakest link was man. Compounded as he was of matter and spirit, he was the place of transition from one world to another, a glorious and tragic denizen of two spheres of existence.

So long as the notion of the chain of being held intellectual sway, man's place within nature as that link in the chain

45

responsible for nature to God, there could be no question of his absolute right over it or its complete objectification. But the break-up of medieval Europe, the decline in the power of the Church, and the new Protestant emphasis upon individual sin and salvation hastened the demise of the medieval doctrine of creation. The genius of Shakespeare, writing with the confident flourish of a Renaissance artist, caught this new sense of man's estrangement from God on the one side and from the natural world on the other.

> What a piece of work is a man! How noble in reason! how infinite in faculty! in form and moving, how express and admirable! in action how like an angel! in apprehension how like a god! the beauty of the world! the paragon of animals. And yet, to me, what is this quintessence of dust? (*Hamlet*, Act II, Sc. 11).

The intellectual revolution of the seventeenth century, with its new questions and answers about man and his place in the universe, marks, as many historians have made clear, the beginning of the modern world.

It was a world in which the empirical sciences were to become more and more influential in the shaping of society and the environment. Early on in that century Francis Bacon had declared that the aim of a scientific understanding of nature was 'the restitution and re-investing (in greater part) of man to the sovereignty and power . . . which he had in his first state of creation'. In this interesting remark he already hints at what was to become a commonplace belief in the secular Western world: that the destiny of man and the making of a better world lay in man's own hands. The realization of the kingdom of God, it could now be seen, was no longer a matter of God's redemptive action, but one of scientific endeavour.

What can be seen in the progress of the seventeenth century is the steady elimination of God from nature. The medieval picture of the ordered, hierarchical, sacramental universe full of the signs of the personal presence of God was destroyed; as was the more primitive biblical picture of the whole of

46

nature as the field of God's glory. The stars no longer sang, the waters no longer blessed, the sun and moon no longer praised their creator, as they had been wont to do, for they had become 'objects' of man's awareness, distinct from him, things 'out there' to be examined, classified and, if possible, used. By the end of the eighteenth century—so swift had been the progress of this thought—a visionary such as William Blake, who denounced John Locke and Isaac Newton and saw God and nature as a single, dynamic whole, was regarded by most people as distinctly odd and by many as half-way to madness.

Throughout the seventeenth and eighteenth centuries there steadily spread the belief that nature, and life, had been demystified. 'The laws of Nature are the laws of reason; they are always and everywhere the same, and like the axioms of mathematics they have only to be presented in order to be acknowledged as just and right by all men' (Willey, p. 10). It was inevitable that a picture of nature as a vast and elaborate machine should come to dominate both the scientific and the popular imagination. This entailed an assumption of the separation of God from his creation: he became the remote, uninterested, original constructor of the mechanism, one who had made its parts and set it in motion and had now withdrawn to allow it to run on its course without further intervention. The way lay open for man's assumption of absolute control over the world. Since God had been eliminated, man was in charge; it was his world and it was his task to repair the machine and make such improvements as he saw fit.

Of course there were spirits like William Blake who looked upon the scientific and technological advances with the greatest foreboding, but the curious fact is that, in the main, religion and science reached an incongruous accommodation in these centuries. The scientists were not irreligious, even if they were making strenuous efforts to exclude the supernatural, and R. S. Westfall in his book *Science and Religion in Seventeenth-Century England* has suggested that there were certain aspects of Protestant thought which actually assisted the adoption of the mechanical picture of the world by scientists who were not at all estranged from religion. 'Particularly in the sermons by John Wallis, the most rigid Calvinist among the English scientists, the image of God as arbitrary will laying down eternal and unchangeable laws for the creation seems ready to merge with Robert Boyle's portrait of the Divine Mechanic constructing his inexorable machine' (p. 5).

I have not the slightest doubt that it is this same picture, tinged, very often, with superstitious apprehensions of the preternatural (belief in ghosts, poltergeists, fortune-telling), which has persisted and prevails in the minds of the vast majority, Christians included, of all those who have been affected by Western culture. Our own century has seen the abandonment of this picture by scientists, but this very significant change of perspective (among physicists and astronomers in particular) has not yet filtered down to influence the life of the layman who, as long as he is captivated by the picture left to him by his ancestors of the Enlightenment and the Industrial Revolution, will continue to look upon nature as something exterior to himself, something to be used and exploited, and he will be ambivalent towards the attempts of modern ecologists to halt the process of the destruction of his environment.

We must return to the question of the relevance of the doctrine of the incarnation to the issue of the relationship between man and nature. I suggest we begin by glancing first at certain aspects of the theology of the Eastern Orthodox Church. One does not need to be a scholar to be aware of the divergence between Eastern and Western interpretations of a number of matters basic to the Christian faith, and one does not need to be a historian to be aware of the fact that the doctrines of creation and incarnation are not only more closely interwoven in Byzantine theology, but also occupy a much more imposing place in the structure of belief and devotion. Dominating the art and theology of Eastern Orthodox Christianity is the figure of Christ as Pantocrator: the agent of creation, the second person of the Holy Trinity, through whom all things in heaven and earth were created

48

and by whom all things are sustained in being. Western Christianity is, of course, a more variegated phenomenon, but even while acknowledging the comparative lack of uniformity, it is not misleading to say that since the time of Augustine of Hippo the central image for faith and devotion has not been the incarnate Word, but the crucified and risen Lord. In saying this I am not arguing that Byzantine theology neglected the human life and the sacrificial death of Jesus Christ or that Western theology (Catholic and Protestant) was not interested in the doctrines of creation and incarnation, but the difference of emphasis is not insignificant: they helped to shape the development of the cultures of East and West and in doing so influenced the ways in which the relationship between man and his natural surroundings were understood.

The great scientific achievements of the Western world, taking place within the religious framework provided by Catholicism and Protestantism, have no parallel in any other culture. Scientific advance in the Byzantine world was negligible, and it could be argued that the Byzantine doctrine of creation would have hampered any movement towards the establishment and growth of any empirical science. The natural world originally created in harmony and order by God was sanctified by him in the incarnation of his Son. With this sanctification the sharp division between what is natural and what is supernatural had been overcome, and Byzantine devotion, both public and private, shows the worshipper moving, it appears, with the greatest of ease between earth and heaven—for the former is contained in the latter. No such ease is generally characteristic of Western devotion. The doctrine of original sin is more deeply dug into Western theology and the separation of the divine and the human is correspondingly wider. The necessity of overcoming this division has meant that faith and devotion has tended to be focused upon the atoning work of Christ. The doctrine of the incarnation, therefore, instead of being united to the doctrine of creation, is linked to theories of atonement, and the event of the incarnation, as I have already indicated in the first chapter, is seen

49

only as a necessary preliminary to the sacrificial death and resurrection of the saviour. Even in the classical Catholic understanding of the relationship between grace and nature—that grace perfects nature without destroying it (*gratia naturam non tollit, sed perfecit*)—one does not gather the sense of the coinherence of the realms of nature and supernature that one gathers in Eastern Orthodoxy. With the coming of the Protestant Reformation grace and nature were thrust even farther apart and the gulf between man and God deepened into a terrifying abyss. The desacralization of nature opened the way that was to lead, eventually, to the removal of the supernatural from the sphere of the natural altogether, and to the consequent 'objectification' of nature.

There is no possibility of such 'objectification' in Byzantine thought. Tracing the development of the doctrine of creation in Byzantine theology, John Meyendorff writes: 'To express the relationship between creator and creation, the great Maximus the Confessor uses the old theology of the Logos as center and living unity of the logos of creation' (p. 132). In this manner the life of the created order is able to participate in the life of the creator. The Logos, the second person of the Trinity and the true image of the Father, becomes in the incarnate Lord Jesus unified with his own creation, vivifying it and sanctifying it in that miraculous union.

Bearing this divergence between East and West in mind, do we find ourselves driven into a curious dilemma as we consider this question of man's relationship to his world? It would seem that in a Christian tradition which has retained, and which strongly emphasizes in its teaching and spirituality, the centrality of the interdependent doctrines of creation and incarnation, the possibility of scientific achievement is limited. The very sense one receives from Byzantine Christianity of the wholeness and holiness of the natural world—to say nothing of the sense of being part of an unchanging historical tradition—seems to discourage those impulses of curiosity and individual endeavour which were vital parts of the scientific revolution of Western Europe. Conversely, in a tradition which had man and his salvation at its centres, which had desacralized nature and lost the sense of the coinherence of the supernatural and the natural, the scientific achievement of Western Europe (which must be regarded as one of the most glorious manifestations of the human spirit) became possible. To pose the question in its crudest terms: can we only have the one at the expense of the other?

Of course, there are many factors, political, demographic, economic, social, which also account for the absence of scientific advance in Byzantium, and it would be foolish to overlook them, just as there are factors other than religious to account for the rise of science in Western Europe; but we cannot ignore the important part played by religion in the shaping of cultures and societies. If we cannot ignore that, then we must acknowledge that the doctrinal tradition of the Church in the West is, in part, responsible for what has happened in the world. And what has happened is the spread of Western European science and technology to its farthest corners. Up until the beginning of the twentieth century this phenomenon would have been regarded by most people as an occasion of rejoicing: it was assumed by most that advanced technology could only enhance the quality of human life. In the last eight decades, however, the picture has changed considerably: advances in technology produce as much fear as delight, and we have begun to see that the immediate enrichment of human life has been at the expense of much of the natural world. The destruction that has already been wrought upon the environment and the even more terrible possibility of what could be wrought by engagement in nuclear wars is causing many to wonder whether the cost has been too great.

In his collection of essays on nuclear warfare, Jonathan Schell ends the second essay with a tentative proposal that a world released from the threat of nuclear destruction involves the acceptance of three principles. It is the third of these which concerns us now.

A third principle would be respect for God or nature, or whatever one chooses to call the universal dust that made, or became us. We need to remember that neither as individuals nor as a species have we created ourselves. And we need to remember that our swollen power is not a power to create but only a power to destroy ... Even our power of destruction is hardly our own. As a fundamental property of matter, nuclear energy was nature's creation, and was only discovered by us ... With respect to creation, things still stand as they have always stood, with extra-human powers performing the miracle, and human beings receiving the fruits (p. 178).

The book is not a Christian nor even a religious tract, but the author here makes a point about Christian doctrine that has not been taken seriously enough by most Christians living in Western civilization. Respect for nature because it is the creation of God and loved by him, not merely for our sake but for its own sake, should be basic to every Christian's understanding of God and the world; yet it is not so. Because the Church in the West has for so long failed to see the centrality of the doctrine of creation in her faith and devotion, it has been left, on the whole, to non-Christian thinkers and organizations to protest against the misuse of the world's resources and the destruction of the environment.

In arguing for the restoration of the doctrine of creation to a central place in Christianity I am not arguing for a return to a pre-mechanical age or for the Church to become aligned with some of the more bizarre activities of those who are concerned about the environment. Christianity is neither Luddite nor Utopian. It is not possible nor desirable to 'unmake' what has already been made in the course of the scientific achievements of the last four centuries; and in a world where moral choices are usually choices between conflicting goods or conflicting evils, the environment can never remain intact. The use of technology will always involve some destruction and loss in the natural order. What can be prevented is wanton destruction: destruction which is caused not because it has been chosen as the lesser of two evils, but because motives of power or greed have overriden the respect due to, and the care of, that which God has created and loved. There

52

is a story told of the author St John Perse. When asked why he had published relatively little in his lifetime, he replied: 'The birth of a book entails the death of a tree. How many books are worth the trees they killed?' This is the enunciation of a moral principle that, I imagine, very few Christian authors have considered; and it is a principle which is based upon a carefully considered attitude to nature. There is a 'doctrine' of creation in it which is higher than the doctrine of creation of most Christians who actually believe in a creator.

The realization that the advances in science and technology have had deleterious effects upon nature has produced strong reactions for over a century—many of which have taken the form of a utopian withdrawal from the world into efforts at the creation of life in a pre-industrial age. The Church cannot be part of this utopianism for, apart from the practical difficulties, it would be the abandoning of nature to a godless fate. A doctrine of God as creator and lover of the world implies the necessity of living in the world and transforming the attitudes of society as a whole to the question of man's relationship with nature.

My concern is to argue that if there is to be a halt to the destruction of our environment and a restoration of the world of nature, then a change must begin in the Church at a fundamental level. Quite simply, the Church should be less concerned about the salvation of souls and more concerned about the sanctification of life or, to be more precisely theological, less concerned about 'justification by faith' and more concerned about 're-creation by grace'; and the re-creation will extend to the whole of the natural order. We are not souls to be plucked from matter on the day of our salvation, we are part of a universe which along with us waits for the consummation that has been promised by God in Christ. At the level of doctrine this means the reintegration of the doctrines of creation, incarnation and atonement. Wholly interdependent, each must be read in terms of the others.

There are indications that this is, indeed, happening. The attempt to integrate the doctrines and to recover a doctrine

53

of creation has been a strain in Anglican theology for the last hundred years. But even in Protestant traditions, which have previously made much of the disinction between grace and nature, some sense of creation as something more than the demonstration of the absolute power of God is being recovered. In *The Protestant Era* Paul Tillich disturbed many members of his own tradition by pointing out what Protestantism had lost in the years it had spent concentrating on the doctrines of revelation and the word. He may have angered many conservative Christians with his views on the interrelation of the supernatural and the natural, but he performed a valuable service for Protestants and Catholics alike by the questions he raised; and they have not been shrugged off by his successors.

Recently Jürgen Moltmann has written of the necessity for recognizing the unity of the *regnum naturae*, the *regnum gratiae* and the *regnum gloriae*. 'Man is not just the creature made in the image of God, standing over against the non-human creation of God as its master; rather he stands together with all other living things in the ongoing process of a creation which is still open and incomplete.' This expression of the notion of man, *at one with the natural order*, moving towards the common destiny of the kingdom of God, coming as it does from the pen of one of the most distinguished contemporary Lutheran theologians, is highly significant. It may well be that Moltmann was drawing out this thought from a concept of biblical eschatology, and perhaps the eighth chapter of Paul's epistle to the Romans was the seed from which it grew, but whatever its ultimate source, it is not far removed in content from an understanding of the process of creation and salvation which was expressed, admittedly in another 'language' and in an entirely different culture, centuries before Lutheranism was born. Focusing on the teachings of Maximus the Confessor (A.D. 580–662), John Meyendorff summarizes the thought of Byzantine theology thus: '. . . the *movement* (kinesis) of creatures is the necessary and natural consequence of their creation by God. God, therefore, in creating the world, placed outside of Himself a system of dynamic beings, which are

54

different from Him in that they change and move towards Him' (p. 133). In teachings such as these, one the expression of an ancient writer, the other the expression of a modern, we may hope to recover the sense of the true beauty, meaning and value of nature and our responsibility towards it. That responsibility will not exclude scientific investigation nor the use of nature by man, but it will exclude the assumption of man's absolute right to exercise power over nature, and thus exclude also its exploitation and abuse.

I have already remarked on the way in which Byzantine theology treats creation and incarnation as interlocking doctrines, and in an earlier chapter I have commended an understanding of the incarnation as the fulfilment of the original creation. The importance of the material universe becomes even greater when this concept is taken seriously. God did not merely make and love the world, he chose to be united with matter in a single person. Nature was not simply the context of a human life and an action of redemption—a frame for the picture of the spirit of Jesus—but

> Here the impossible union
> Of spheres of existence is actual.
> (T. S. Eliot, *Four Quartets*)

The Jesus who is crucified is also the Logos of God: through him all things come into being, in him all things are 'summed up', and by him all things are sanctified by the presence of his Spirit. In taking man to himself, he takes all nature to himself. Some such vision of the inclusion of the world in Christ and the energizing of that world by the power of his Spirit must have been in the mind of Teilhard de Chardin when he wrote:

As a consequence of Incarnation, the divine immensity has transformed itself for us into *the omnipresence of christification*. All good that I can do *opus et operatio* is physically gathered in, by the reality of the consummated Christ ... Quite specifically it is *Christ whom we make or we undergo in all things (Le Milieu Divin,* p. 123).

Some such vision must also have been in the mind of the author of the epistle to the Colossians when he wrote: 'All things were created through him and for him. He is before all things, and in him all things hold together' (1:16).

Chapter 4

THE WORLD OF ART

There is a terse and bitter remark attributed to the German philosopher, Theodor Adorno: 'After Auschwitz, no poetry!' It gives perfect expression to the almost universally felt sense of incongruity between the horror and waste of the concentration camps of Hitler's Germany (and Stalin's Russia) and the beauty and order which manifest themselves in art. The implication seems clear: art of whatever kind—music, poetry, painting, dancing—is too fragile and ephemeral a human occupation to survive the blast of the brutal reality of human existence. At best, it is a luxury, and in times of growing inhumanity and barbarism like our own, it is shown up as having little force or purpose; at worst, it is a lie, pretending that beauty and order really do exist. The problem may be put quite simply in a different way. A third of the world's population is near to starving, ruinous wars are continually being fought, the resources of the earth are being wasted; have we got the time or the right to compose piano sonatas or paint pictures? Jesus's answer to the devil, 'Man shall not live by bread alone but by every word that proceeds out of the mouth of God', may be neatly balanced by Bertolt Brecht's caustic comment, *'Erst kommt das Fressen, dann kommt die Moral'*: 'Grub first, then ethics.' The only attitude that is proper to assume is, perhaps, one of silence, and any attempt by the artist to break into 'speech' will be ludicrous and meaningless. It is as though, with the disintegration of Western culture, life has gone too far for art, and the population had better use only trivial entertainment to divert its attention, temporarily, from the outrage of existence.

The crisis is felt in all branches of the arts, but most agonizingly by those who are most concerned with 'meaning' because their art is the art of language: poets, novelists, playwrights. Samuel Beckett may stand as one whose awareness of this crisis has consistently provided him with the basic material for his plays. His may be the bleakest vision, but his is one which articulates what many others only have the courage to suggest. The situation and dialogue of an early play like *Waiting for Godot* have given way, in later years, to more absurd locations and increasingly hermetic utterances. A solitary actor conducts a bizarre conversation with his recorded voice; characters sit in dustbins or buried up to their necks in sand mouthing apparent gibberish. As spectators we may react irritably or laughingly; we may be disturbed; we may wonder whether the playwright is mocking us or has simply gone mad. Has the vehicle of language collapsed under the strain of the crisis? Has the time really come for art to cease, except as a private indulgence, because it is not a serious enough activity in a desperately serious time?

Hans Küng has tried to answer this question in a small book called *Art and the Question of Meaning* (1980). He too refers to Theodor Adorno and quotes the philosopher's cryptic assertion: 'Even before Auschwitz, in face of historical experiences, it was an affirmative lie to ascribe to existence any meaning at all (which might have had) consequences even for the form of the work of art' (p. 31). The point being made is that a work of art can define meaninglessness in such a way that it gives the appearance (the affirmative lie) of inward form or 'harmoniousness'. Its meaning is enclosed in its own form and is not the result of its having captured a meaning from the world outside. (Perhaps the peculiar poignancy of Noel Coward's love songs—'I'll see you again', 'Someday I'll find you'—comes from the fact that they are 'affirmative lies'. We, and the composer, know perfectly well that the world is not full of sweetness and possibilities for love to triumph, but harsh, ugly and full of pain; so harsh, indeed, that the only thing we can do is to sing about it as though it were not so.) Needless to say Küng, while sympathetic to the pessimism of Adorno, is concerned to show that the world does have meaning and that works of art are attempts in colour, line, words, movement, sound to grasp and convey that meaning '. . . without superficial optimism, without any affirmative lie; therefore, instead of a basic mistrust, there can be a *basic trust*. And he [the artist] can give expression to this basic trust in art . . .' (p. 32). So art can become, even in these terrible times, a means of allowing us to 'perceive something of the all-embracing dimensions of the mystery which surrounds us'; a way of entering and revealing the mystery which surrounds us and sustains us.

It is an attractive book; one which takes the crisis of culture in the Western world with proper seriousness, but one which also shows a hopefulness which is grounded in a belief in the power of humanity to overcome inhumanity, and in the promise of God for the future of the world. Yet nevertheless, Küng does not ultimately persuade us (perhaps it was not his intention) of the necessity of art. We are given art as elevating, art as stimulus, art as encouragement, art as revelation; but not, quite, art as necessity for human life. I shall be putting forward a case for going further than Küng, and arguing that where our understanding of life is founded in a belief in the incarnation, art—even those piano sonatas and landscapes (for I am not speaking about ecclesiastical art)—are *necessary*.

Leo Tolstoy said as much when he claimed, to the disgust of the aesthetes of his own generation, that art was not to be confused with pleasure, but was 'a means of union among men, joining them together in the same feelings, and indispensable for the life and progress towards well-being of individuals and humanity' (*What is Art?*, p. 50). This is an argument for the necessity of art on the grounds that it is useful. Its function is to help to create a society which is more peaceful, more harmonious, more loving, more united. Art may indeed perform this function: refine feelings, cultivate sensibility, move individuals to act with greater generosity and sympathy; but there is no guarantee that it will do so. It has often been pointed out that the music and poetry enjoyed by the guards of the Nazi concentration camps did nothing to inspire them to act with greater generosity or sympathy towards their unhappy captives, who shared with them a similar love of the arts. It is impossible to make a case for the necessity of art purely on the grounds of its moral effect, as though art, like vitamins or fibre in a diet, would inevitably improve the health of a nation.

We must go behind the problem of effect (for it is a problem) to ask how it is that in every culture of which we have knowledge, there have appeared artefacts that seem to aspire to beauty and form. It is clear that the 'why' of art is a mystery; and throughout history thinkers have found it easier to answer the question 'what is art?', difficult though that is, than the question 'why is art?' Up until the seventeenth century such answers as we were given to the latter question nearly always supposed that there was a connection between art and the realm of the divine. The gift to create was something that came from outside: from God, or the muses; it was therefore inexplicable. This notion has been extraordinarily persistent, despite the scientific revolution of the seventeenth century and the steady secularization of Western culture. It was with the introduction of the mechanical model of the universe and, in subsequent centuries, with the growth of rationalist and idealist philosophies, that other explanations for the genesis of art began to appear.

If man was part of the machine of the world then his ability to make things of order and beauty could not come directly from God (or the muses); the creative impulse had to have its source in the mind or emotions of the autonomous human being. He was not in contact with the divine, he was simply doing the thing he was constructed to do. With the acceptance of psychology as a science other explanations were offered: art was, perhaps, a pathological product, the result of the neurosis of the artist, the exteriorization of a mental disturbance. But the agnostic psychologists by no means had it all their own way, and in 1930 C. G. Jung reverted to the transcendental mode when he wrote:

A person must pay dearly for the divine gift of creative fire.

60

It is as though each of us was born with a limited source of energy. In the artist, the strongest force in his make-up, that is, his creativeness, will seize and all but monopolize this energy, leaving so little over that nothing of value can come of it (p. 207).

Unfortunately there is no space here to examine the numerous theories that have been advanced in the last three centuries to explain the fact of art, but it is interesting to note how resistant artists themselves have been to the idea that the compulsion they feel to create can be explained by the arrangement of their genes or the pressures of their environment. The mystery persists, and they persist in regarding their talents for painting, writing, composing as gifts; and a gift is something received, not something which can be willed out of the self or explained by reference to the internal physical and mental constituents of the creator. The efforts of behavioural psychologists and determinist philosophers have not succeeded in purging our language of the stubbornly transcendental word 'inspiration'; and I do not believe that its continued life is an otiose remnant of a more primitive stage of human development which will wither when we 'come of age'.

But we must be careful when we talk about artistic creation in these transcendental terms. There is, undeniably, a 'visionary' element in all genuine art: the artist 'sees' things others do not see. In its creation there is the perception of beauty and order which is hidden or, at best, dimly perceived by those of us who are not artists. In this 'visionary' sense art is a kind of revelation, so we may be tempted to agree with George MacDonald's description of the task of the poet when he says:

In every man there is an inner chamber of peculiar life into which God alone may enter. There is also a chamber in God himself into which none may enter but the one, the peculiar man—out of which chamber that man has to bring revelation and strength to his brethren. That is that for which he was made—to reveal the secret things of the Father (quoted by W. H. Auden in *Secondary Worlds*, p. 131).

Are we to suppose that there are not others—preachers, mystics, teachers—who reveal 'the secret things of the Father'? If this were so then the artist would indeed be indispensable, for he would be the ultimate channel of the revelation of divine truth like the prophets of ancient Israel, and our question about the place and purpose of art would immediately, and simply, be answered.

I suggest that when this concept of art is stressed it verges on dangerous romanticism and turns art into something it is not. If we believed this we should, in fact, be very close to believing Shelley's grandiose dictum that poets are 'the unacknowledged legislators of the world'. If the artist does exercise a prophetic role, he exercises it differently from the prophets of Israel. And, in any case, an artist does not create because he feels himself in direct contact with the Almighty—not even the icon painter in the Byzantine church, who only begins to work after much preparation in private prayer and public worship. Furthermore, if the impulse to create did come, as prophetic utterance in Israel came, from the conviction of direct contact, all art would be identifiably religious art. It would have as its only subject religious experience.

I may well be distorting the meaning of MacDonald's statement. If it was not intended to identify the role of the artist with that of the prophet, perhaps we might take it to be a rather exaggerated way of pointing to the visionary character of art, and also a way of saying that the response of a person to the revelation of God, as well as his own understanding of himself and the world he inhabits, is occluded, unformed and unsure until the artist reveals it to him. The artist's prime task then is the articulation of the human response to what has already been given by God. So, for example, as we look at the famous painting called *Pieta* from the school of Avignon *c.* 1460, we find that what the artist has done in line and colour is to articulate our hitherto cloudy awareness of some of the meanings of the death of Christ. We may be moved by the sorrow of the mother bending over the body of her son; we see also the abandonment and desolation of all humanity in this death. We do not learn new facts about God here, we learn new things about ourselves. Or, to take another example, our fumbling attempts to understand what it is we feel and see when occasionally we are seized and held by an inexplicable delight in some beauty of the natural world are articulated by Wordsworth in the opening lines of his *Ode: Intimations of Immortality of Early Childhood*. It is important, when we are thinking about this visionary quality of art, and are tempted to use the vocabulary of transcendence, to remember Charles Williams's remark that

> Poetry [all art, even music], one way or another, is 'about' human experience; there is nothing else it can be about. But to whatever particular human experience it alludes, it is not that experience. Love poetry is poetry, not love; patriotic poetry is poetry, not patriotism; religious poetry is poetry, not religion (*A Note on Great Poetry*).

The artist articulates for others experiences they could not articulate for themselves, and also awakens in others an awareness of their own capacity for new experience. Art, therefore, is not 'about' God, even when the incarnate Lord is its subject: it is 'about' man, and it is the way of acquiring a special kind of self-knowledge.

No, it cannot be on the basis of a prophetic role that art must be regarded as a necessity of man's life and one of the means of renewing the world. None the less our basis for arguing for its necessity is religious. For us, the answer to the question 'Why is art?' lies in our understanding of the nature of God, of his creative activity and particularly of that event we call the incarnation. My argument is that the creation of works of art is the inevitable response of the human race to a religious fact. The conditions of man's creation are such that he cannot be other than an artist.

When theologians of the nineteenth and twentieth centuries tried to eradicate the deistic conceptions of creation—that God had constructed the world as a vast machine and then left it to go on running according to the inbuilt laws of its construction—they first dismantled the analogy of God as the machine-maker, and many of them put in its place the analogy of God as the artist. This brought God into more intimate contact with his world. The analogy was particularly popular among English thinkers. Oliver C. Quick's influential book *Doctrines of the Creed*, first published in 1938, contains a well-known chapter which describes the way an artist expresses his real self in his work; is involved with it, loves it and delights in it. So, Quick argues, God,

> since he creates out of the infinite resources of his own being, all things in various manners and degrees of perfection express him. It is thus that the artistic analogy leads us towards a conception of divine immanence which the analogy of the craftsman or machine-maker could not suggest (p. 45).

In an even better-known book, *The Mind of the Maker*, Dorothy L. Sayers makes the analogy of the artist the basis for her exposition of the most fundamental of all Christian doctrines, that of the Trinity. 'Thus Berdyaev is able to say: "God created the world by imagination." This experience of the creative imagination in the common man or woman and in the artist is the only thing we have to go on in entertaining and formulating the concept of creation' (p. 23). But the idea is not confined to English theology. Jacques Maritain considered it in *Art and Scholasticism*, and in recent years a much subtler, more comprehensive (and, it must be admitted, more difficult) development has appeared in the German Catholic tradition in the work of the Swiss theologian Hans Urs von Balthasar. For him all beauty, whether its forms are natural or man-made, confronts human beings with 'the radiance of the Incarnate Word himself'.

Of course, the creative activity of God can and must be described by the use of analogies other than this one, but this has a unique power: it chimes with the human being's own emotional and psychological experience in creating something, however humble. It is in the activity of the imagin-

64

ation—of bringing into being, by a combination of mental energy and technical skill, things that previously had no existence—that the individual feels most 'god-like'. It is an experience of release from the constrictions of the self; and it is experienced at all levels of life: from the child daubing with a paint-brush to the composer producing a symphony. This transcendental experience gives content to the belief that man is made in the image of God. I am not arguing that it exhausts the content, that this is the *only* interpretation of the doctrine; I am simply remarking on its peculiar power and meaning, and saying that it is of particular significance for us as we consider man's own capacity to create 'secondary worlds' by his art and craft. In saying that, if we believe man is made in God's image, however marred that image may be by sin, we must believe that he is primarily, and necessarily, a creator. It implies that art is no luxury to be enjoyed when the human race has the time for the enjoyment of such ephemeral pleasures, but essential to his being.

Paradoxically, artistic creation has the appearance of gratuitousness. Man, as a species, need not create works of art in order to survive; he could remain imaginatively passive and 'dumb' in the world he has been given. It is obvious that painting, dancing, music are not essential to his existence in the way that eating, drinking, sleeping and copulating are. But it is precisely here, at this point of apparent gratuitousness, that man becomes man and is distinguished from the rest of the created order. It is only the species, man, which is made in the image of God, and neither the angels nor the animals possess the gift of that gratuitous action which we call artistic creation.

Thomas Aquinas, along with most medieval theologians, maintained that only mankind was capable of discursive thought. This implied the use of words for the formulation of that thought. The angels, being purely spiritual, did not speak, but communicated by direct 'mental' apprehension; the animals communicated by sense and instinct only. But man, composed as he was of matter and spirit, possessed the unique gift. We may drive the argument beyond the terms and conclusions of medieval theology and say that if the capacity to speak is the essential mark of man's differentiation from all other forms of created life, then that capacity is the basis for all art. Language is not merely a means of communication, a sophisticated development of the complex systems of communication to be observed in the animal world; it is a means of self-expression and self-awareness, a means of laying hold upon ourselves as individuals, a means, almost, of bringing ourselves into conscious being. I am not proposing to open up the debate on which comes first, words or thoughts, but I am saying that without being able to say who we are, we should not be able to know who we are or even, perhaps, to know *that* we are. 'I establish and preserve my experience of self by a stream of internalized address. . . . We do not speak *to ourselves* so much as *speak ourselves*' (Steiner, p. 64). The words we use are the symbols that give shape and meaning to the inchoate reality of our lives. Without that capacity to externalize ourselves in symbols, and by so doing to reflect upon that reality, we should simply be animals. Art is nothing more (and nothing less) than the extension—in many different material forms—of that fundamental image/symbol-making capacity. In art man is detached from himself in order that he may know himself. The art he creates is the symbol, the image, of his own, not God's, hidden interior world. It is, of course, true that while every human being has the capacity to make symbols for himself, they are usually inadequate, and only a few individuals have the imaginative power to form universal symbols: artistic masterpieces wherein all other human beings are able to 'read' the meaning of their own existences.

There we might be content to leave the matter, assured that art is not only enjoyable and valuable and, even, instructive, but natural to man and indispensable. However, I wrote earlier that the 'why' of art lies in our Christian understanding of God not only as creator but also as incarnate, so I turn now to the way in which a belief in the incarnation affects our understanding of the necessity of art. The connection between art and the incarnation has been disappointingly

66

dealt with by Christian thinkers. Most of those who have raised it have acknowledged that there is a connection, but they seldom pursue it.

Even William Neil, in an essay in which we might have expected an exposition, *Christianity and the Arts*, disappoints us when he is content to say what has always been said:

> But of course for the Christian it is above all the fact of the Incarnation that proclaimed the intrinsic worth of the arts and their status as an essential part of the human scene and the enrichment of the human mind. We live on a visited planet. The Son of God came among men as a craftsman and a teacher making the common things of life holy and secular things sacred. The gulf has been bridged between God and man, for Christ made the earth the fore-court of heaven. The world around us reflects the glory of God and the Christian artist whether he works with words or harmonies, with canvas, wood or stone, interprets his vision of God's glory for the enrichment of men's minds and the beautification of their environment in obedience to the declared purpose of God in Christ to transform and renew the whole life of man, beginning here and now (p. 22).

All this is true and it is well said. The taking of human flesh by God for once and for all forbids man to look upon his body as the brutal cage of the unhappy soul or to regard matter as though it were, at best, a mistake or, at worst, evil. The union of God and man in Jesus Christ sets the seal of God's approval upon human beings taking the things of this world and mould-ing them in ways that enable matter to become the vehicle for the transmission of the glory of its creator. From the very earliest days Christianity has maintained this position, and maintained it in the teeth of the repeated onslaughts of Gnos-ticism—in all its guises—which, with its profound distrust of matter, has attempted the overthrow of the realm of art.

We cannot, however, leave the matter there, for the argu-ment, true as it is, does not go far enough; it does not offer us a reason why man must, of necessity, express his visions

67

in 'words or harmonies ... canvas, wood or stone'. The incarnation, by this argument, allows for such things to happen as a delightful enrichment of man's life, but still does not demand that it should be placed centrally there. In order to understand why it is central, and not merely an adornment, we might refer to some words of Gerardus van der Leeuw, who is one of the few theologians who take us further than the generalized statements of Neil. He writes: 'It can and must be possible to recognise in the beautiful work of man the features of the work of God, since God himself gave to his earthly creation the features of his own image' (p. 339). It is those last six words which are important and whose meaning we must now pursue.

I have already tried to show, in the first chapter of this book, how it is possible to see the incarnation not merely as the necessary prelude to the drama of the atonement, but as the culmination of God's creative action and the ultimate revelation and communication of himself. To be sure, the creative action took into itself the redemption of man, and the revelation was the revelation of God who both loves and saves, but it was also, and vitally, the revelation of the mystery of the Trinity: a revelation that it was (and is) God *as Trinity* who creates and redeems. This is the fundamental doctrine of Christianity and a proper understanding of man and the creative processes of his imagination will only be reached when the truth of the doctrine is recognized.

Donald McKinnon is not the only theologian to notice the paradox that at the present time, when there is 'great interest in the characteristically Christian doctrine of God', this interest is frequently accompanied 'by a certain impatience with the doctrine of the Trinity' (p. 103). Both Karl Rahner and Jürgen Moltmann have drawn attention to the dead hand of 'unitarianism' which has held Christianity in its stony grip for centuries. 'One could suspect that as regards the catechism of the head and the heart, in contrast to the catechism in books, the Christian idea of the Incarnation would not have to change at all, if there were no Trinity' (vol. iv, p. 80). I have little doubt that most readers coming across those words of Rahner will immediately recognize their truth. The intimate connection between the two doctrines is almost never stressed. Private devotion is usually directed either to an undifferentiated 'God' or to the person of Jesus or, less frequently, to the Holy Spirit, the relation between them only formally acknowledged. When the incarnation is spoken of in the pulpit it is usually presented in the generalities of God becoming man, seldom in the specificities of the Word (the second person of the Godhead) becoming flesh. The precise doctrine of the Trinity whose persons are eternally separate and eternally united is avoided as difficult and obscure, remote and apparently self-contradictory; and when it is presented it is often produced as an arithmetical conundrum. There is the faintly embarrassed and apologetic air of someone who has inherited an awkward piece of furniture from a long-dead relative: it seems to have value, but it does not have much use, a relic of an earlier age which is difficult to store in the room of one's faith. I have no doubt that this pervasive 'unitarianism' of Western Christendom has helped to make the doctrine of the incarnation, about which there has been so much controversy of late, seem more implausible. Isolated from the concept of the Father's personal communication of himself in his Word, who in becoming man reveals and communicates the Father to his creation, the doctrine of the incarnation appears unnecessary. When the doctrine of the Trinity is seen only as a metaphysical speculation unconnected to the grace and salvation offered by God, then the historical Christ becomes a kind of divine person hovering awkwardly between heaven and earth.

We still have to show the relevance of the Christian belief in the Triune God to our understanding of man as artist. In the making of a work of art the human being, as I have said, exercises a peculiar kind of mental and emotional energy. It is a drive to externalize; a compulsion to express, to symbolize, to embody in material forms the visions of his interior 'eye': his imagination. This energetic expression is nothing less than the reflection of the divine life of the Trinity. As we consider the meaning of the statement that man is made in

69

the image of God it becomes apparent that the image is not merely the image of a God in a unitarian monotheistic religion, not even the image of the Creator/Father God of the Old Testament. The revelation of Christ in the New Testament, which is that of a life lived by the Son of God in the power of the Spirit, is the revelation of exchanged love and creative energy within the Godhead himself. So the image in which man is made is that of the Triune God of the Christian gospel.

This does not mean that we are forced to say, naively, that every human being is a copy of God in the possession of three distinct elements (body, mind, spirit), but we are enabled to talk of a recognizable correspondence between the life of God and the life of man, and see what should be clear: '. . . the true mode of human existence is that which resembles God' (van der Leeuw, p. 324). This correspondence and resemblance is to be perceived chiefly in the eternal self-expression of the Father in his Son or Word, and the self-knowledge eternally received in the flowing backwards and forwards, in and out, of the Spirit. In man there is this same drive to self-expression and necessity for self-knowledge, however darkened and distorted by sin, which is at the basis of all art.

At the risk of writing crudely and anthropomorphically, I would say that just as man remains mute and ignorant without that explosion of energy which we call art, so the Father remains mute and unknowing until he has expressed himself in his Word.

> Here again we can discover in our art as it were a trace of the Blessed Trinity. *The Word*, says St Augustine, *is in a way the art of Almighty God*. And by the Word the whole divine work was done, *omnia per ipsum facta sunt*. It is through His Word and His art that God attains, controls and realises, everything He does (Maritain, p. 132).

It is the unique insight of Christianity (or the unique *gift* of Christianity, since it has come by way of revelation) to perceive that God in his supreme energy is both utterly still and constantly moving. The Father does not reign self-contained, self-sufficient, self-engrossed; but eternally moves out of himself into his Son and receives himself in his Spirit. He puts himself forth in his Word, the personal expression of his being, and receives himself personally in his Spirit. But it is his Son, his Word, who is his very image, his 'real symbol'.

Since, therefore, self-expressive energy has been revealed to us as the absolutely necessary structure of the life of God, it cannot be an activity which is optional in the life of man. Art is as necessary to humanity as speech. So man, whose very nature has been newly created in the risen and glorified Christ, embodies himself in his own creations by the power of the incarnate Word, and 'reads' himself back in the power of the Holy Spirit. He will not know who he is, nor why he is, until he has done so.

So far I have deliberately said very little about a subject most people would have expected to find in a discussion like this: the connection between art and beauty. This is partly because the notion of 'the beautiful' is so complicated that if it were to be properly discussed it would have required a whole book and not a chapter. But it cannot be completely ignored, for in the minds of nearly everyone there is an indissoluble association between beauty and art. The outrage which is caused by so much modern art is not merely because the mass of people are conservative and resent new works for being strange, untraditional and upsetting, but because the new works do not seem to conform to some standard of 'the beautiful'. The accusation of an offended public is not only that the new things are strange but that they are ugly. The criteria upon which judgements are made are usually extraordinarily shaky, for it is a simple fact that standards of beauty do not remain constant. Rachmaninov's first symphony and Stravinsky's *Rite of Spring*, for example, were both greeted with derision and execration when they were first performed, yet today they are accepted not only as 'artistic' but as 'beautiful'.

Granted that the notion of beauty is so volatile, so that the appreciation of something is intensely subjective and liable to change, it is remarkable that the concept of beauty still exists.

71

One could argue that the word 'beauty' is nothing more than a sound human beings make when they experience a certain kind of mental and emotional satisfaction, and one would find that a difficult proposition to refute. But whence the desire for this kind of satisfaction, and why should it be particularly associated with art? The answer, again, is found in what we have already discussed: the revelation of God as Trinity, the incarnation of the Word, and the creation of man in the image of his creator.

God is beauty itself and the cause of all beauty in his creatures. *Ex divina pulchritudine esse omnium derivatur.* But, because God is triune there is more to be said, and Maritain has reminded us that Thomas Aquinas said it when he perceived that 'In the trinity . . . the title Beauty is specially appropriate to the Son . . . the light and splendour of the mind [of the Father]' (p. 32). It is the Son, the perfectly beautiful image of the Father, who unites himself to his material world and takes human form; a form of lowliness and humility, but one which contains the splendour of the Godhead. Thus, the eternal Word, agent of the Father's creativity, is the source of all beauty in creation, however variously it is presented and perceived. It is, perhaps, the recognition of this truth that lies behind the profound but somewhat enigmatic statement of Balthasar that was quoted earlier: in all forms of beauty human beings are confronted with 'the radiance of the Incarnate Word himself'.

If the Spirit of God is to renew the world and act through human beings in doing so, this action of renewal will not be achieved without the work of the artist, however far he may be from the Church and the making of ecclesiastical images. Art is the consequence of man's being made in God's image and the image of God who is the Word himself, incarnate in Jesus Christ, crucified and risen; so all genuine art is Christian art. It may not be liturgical or biblical; it may be dramatic, choreographic, musical, poetic. It may take a hundred forms and be responded to in a thousand ways, but it will be Christian. It may not increase good works or encourage repentance, but it will have its origin in the Word of God.

72

'. . . Wherever art, Egyptian, Greek or Chinese, has attained a certain degree of grandeur and purity, it is already Christian, Christian in hope, because every spiritual splendour is a promise and a symbol of the divine harmonies of the Gospel' (Maritain, p. 69).

EPILOGUE

It will have become apparent, by now, how difficult it has been to take a subject like 'the renewal of the world' and say something meaningful and coherent about it. The difficulty arises, partly, out of trying to find the meaning of the word 'world', and I am sure that I have slipped and slid between a number of definitions in the previous chapters. There is, unfortunately, no definition provided by any of the writers of the New Testament to whom the idea of and belief in such a renewal is basic to their idea of and belief in Christ. We could retreat into an apocalypticism and not go beyond saying that the new world promised by the Messiah will be inaugurated by God only after death and the dissolution of this present order; that could be the view of the author of the *Revelation to John*. But to most of the other writers of the New Testament the renewal of life and of the world seems to have been seen as something which began to take place with the coming of Jesus and could be observed in the present.

Nineteen centuries later Karl Marx was convinced that such talk about renewal was nothing but a lie and proposed methods by which the lie could be exposed. When that was done a really new world could be gained. As the years pass and communist regimes show no signs of becoming less oppressive and brutal than the autocratic or democratic systems they were supposed to replace, Marx's solutions seem less and less convincing and the methods he proposed more and more dubious.

But who, looking around the world as it is today with a sensitive eye, will find the evidence to refute Marx's passionate statement of disaffection with the achievements of Christian civilization? On every side we see signs of political cynicism and social despair; we see the remorseless destruction of the beauty of the natural world and the mindless waste of natural resources; we see the kind of disintegration of culture that makes the work of the artist seem trivial, meaningless or mad. Anthony Burgess, an acute observer of contemporary mores, ended his review of *A Dictionary of Contemporary Quotations* in *The Observer* newspaper of 29 August 1982 with the words: 'We're living in a very cynical world, also sentimental, also ill-educated, also vulgar.' If Burgess is right and the book under review can be taken as some kind of index of the state of the world, then where do we look for renewal and how dare we, as Christians, hope for renewal?

We may, like many of our contemporaries, admit that Christianity has run its course and had its day. Its myths have been discredited and can no longer sustain the civilization they created. Out of the ashes of the old religion must grow something new: a religion without myth or ritual, a way of life without dogma, a faith without illusions. Contemporary despair will be met with this new hope. I take Don Cupitt's most recent book to be an expression of this new hope, and his reluctant farewell to Christianity with its myths and rituals, its dogmas and 'illusions'. The old 'climate', which was capable of sustaining so much life, has changed and we must learn to breathe a new air. 'How are we to live in this climate? Four guiding principles become fundamental: truth, disinterestedness, creativity and love' (p. 150). With these principles and without a God to adore we should be equipped to survive our altered conditions. There is nothing timid, fearful or ignoble in Cupitt's prescription for living, and it has been held by many down the ages who found they could not believe in man's 'supernatural existential'. If I could go by a way in which there is no ecstasy to a place in which there is no ecstasy, then I should choose this. If I could believe that morals could replace metaphysics and still satisfy the human spirit, then I should believe this. If I had not discovered that life was pointless and painful one moment and shot through

76

with inexplicable splendour the next, I should want to live after this manner. If I could accept that this answered the paradox with which I began this book, then I should accept it. But I cannot. In fact, I find its supposedly 'thin and bracing' air cheerless and dank as though blowing from a pit of cold resignation. Its reasonableness and fortitude do not reach down to touch the deepest yearnings of my heart or the unceasing restlessness of my spirit. Give me rather the 'absurd' philosophy of Albert Camus, for it touches more nearly the core of my being than this way in which there is neither height nor depth.

A paradox is where we start from, and ours is not an easy journey: orthodoxy with 'its faith in the resurrection of Christ and its constant peering into the future to the coming resurrection of the dead and the transcendental transformation of heaven and earth, has always hampered the true work of orthopraxis and the immanent transformation of the world' (Balthasar, *Elucidations*, p. 194). But the journey can be entered on with hope, whatever false starts have been made in the past. It must be remembered that the gospel of Christ never promised an earthly paradise: the realization of a utopian dream. Its promise was of a future in which the whole world would be taken into the glory of God. 'When all things are subjected to him, then the Son himself will also be subjected to him who put all things under him, that God may be everything to every one' (1 Cor 15:28). It did not give details of when this would be or how this would be. It did not merely propose a state of bliss in a world after death, but it promised a way out of that dilemma which is posed by the contradiction of death. It did not give us permission to vault over the present in order to arrive at the future, it laid upon us the obligation of living as though that future had arrived and to shape our lives in accordance with the joyful expectation of its consummation. It told us that the guarantee of the promise for the future lay in the past, in the single event which was the true symbol of the end: the union of all things in God, the incarnation.

77

BIBLIOGRAPHY

Aquinas, Thomas, *Summa Theologica*, tr. the English Dominican Fathers. R. and T. Washbourne 1912.

Arendt, H., *Men in Dark Times*. Penguin Books 1973.

Auden, W. H., *Secondary Worlds*. Faber & Faber 1968.

Balthasar, H. Urs von, *Engagement with God*. Burns & Oates 1972. *Elucidations*. SPCK 1975.

Camus, A., *The Myth of Sisyphus and Other Essays*. Penguin Modern Classics 1979.

Carson, R., *Silent Spring*. Houghton Mifflin 1962.

Crites, S., *In the Twilight of Christendom*. Chambersbury, Penn., American Academy of Religion, 1972.

Cupitt, D., *The World to Come*. SCM Press 1982.

Elliott-Binns, L. E., *English Thought, 1860–1900*. Longmans 1956.

Jung, C. G., *Psychological Reflections*, sel. and ed. J. Jacobi. Routledge & Kegan Paul 1953.

Küng, H., *Art and the Question of Meaning*. SCM Press 1981.

McKinnon, D. M., 'Relations of Doctrines of Incarnation and Trinity,' in *Creation, Christ and Culture*, ed. McKinney. T. & T. Clark 1976.

Maritain, J., *Art and Scholasticism*. Sheed & Ward 1935.

Marx, K., *Selected Writings*, ed. D. McLellan. OUP 1978.

Meyendorff, J., *Byzantine Theology*. Mowbrays 1974.

Moltmann, J., 'Creation and Redemption' in *Creation, Christ and Culture*, ed. McKinney. T. & T. Clark 1976.

Newton, E. and Neil, W., *The Christian Faith in Art*. Hodder & Stoughton 1966.

Quick, O. C., *Doctrines of the Creed*. Nisbet 1946.

Rahner, K., *Theological Investigations*. Darton, Longman & Todd 1961—.

Sayers, D. L., *The Mind of the Maker*. Methuen 1941.

Schell, J., *The Fate of the Earth*. Picador 1982.

Shook, L. K., *Theology of Renewal*, vol. ii. Herder & Herder 1968.

Steiner, G., *Extra-territorial*. Faber & Faber 1972.

Stern, K., *Pillar of Fire*. Michael Joseph 1951.

Tolstoy, L., *What is Art?* Walter Scott Ltd 1899.

Van der Leeuw, G., *Sacred and Profane Beauty*. Weidenfeld & Nicholson 1963.

Westcott, B. F., 'The Gospel of Creation' in *The Epistles of St John*. Macmillan 1886.

Westfall, R. S., *Science and Religion in Seventeenth-century England*. Yale University Press 1958.

Willey, B., *The Eighteenth-century Background*. Penguin Books 1972.

Williams, C. W. S., *Selected Writings*, ed. Anne Ridler. OUP 1961.

Wordsworth, W., *Poems*. J. M. Dent 1955.